Inside the Earth

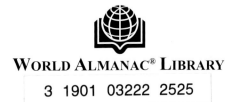

WORLD ALMANAC® LIBRARY

Please visit our web site at: www.worldalmanaclibrary.com
For a free color catalog describing World Almanac® Library's list of high-quality books
and multimedia programs, call 1-800-848-2928 (USA) or 1-800-461-9120 (Canada).
World Almanac® Library's Fax: (414) 332-3567.

The editors at World Almanac® Library would like to thank Paul Mayer, Geology Collections
Manager, Milwaukee Public Museum, for the technical expertise and advice he brought to
the production of this book.

Library of Congress Cataloging-in-Publication Data

Inside the earth. — North American ed.
     p. cm. — (21st century science)
    Includes bibliographical references and index.
    ISBN 0-8368-5002-5 (lib. bdg.)
    1. Geology—Juvenile literature. [1. Earth. 2. Geology.] I. Title.
  II. Series.
  QE29.I57   2001
  550—dc21   2001031094

This North American edition first published in 2001 by
World Almanac® Library
330 West Olive Street, Suite 100
Milwaukee, WI 53212 USA

Created and produced as the *Visual Guide to Understanding the Earth* by
QA INTERNATIONAL
329 rue de la Commune Ouest, 3ᵉ étage
Montreal, Québec
Canada H2Y 2E1
Tel: (514) 499-3000 Fax: (514) 499-3010
www.qa-international.com

© QA International, 2001

Editorial Director: François Fortin
Executive Editor: Serge D'Amico
Illustrations Editor: Marc Lalumière
Art Director: Rielle Lévesque
Graphic Designer: Anne Tremblay
Writers: Nathalie Fredette, Stéphane Batigne, Josée Bourbonnière, Claude Lafleur,
Agence Science-Presse
Computer Graphic Artists: Jean-Yves Ahern, Maxime Bigras, Patrice Blais, Yan Bohler,
Mélanie Boivin, Charles Campeau, Jocelyn Gardner, Jonathan Jacques, Alain Lemire,
Raymond Martin, Nicolas Oroc, Carl Pelletier, Simon Pelletier, Frédérick Simard,
Mamadou Togola, Yan Tremblay
Page Layout: Lucie Mc Brearty, Véronique Boisvert, Geneviève Théroux Béliveau
Researchers: Anne-Marie Villeneuve, Anne-Marie Brault, Kathleen Wynd, Jessie Daigle
Earth Reviewer: Michèle Fréchet
Copy Editor: Liliane Michaud
Production: Mac Thien Nguyen Hoang
Prepress: Tony O'Riley
World Almanac® Library Editor: David K. Wright
World Almanac® Library Art Direction: Karen Knutson
Cover Design: Katherine A. Kroll

Photo credits: abbreviations: t = top, c = center, b = bottom, r = right, l = left
p. 31 (tl): Ed Wolfe, United States Department of the Interior, USGS, David A. Johnston
Cascades Volcano Observatory, Vancouver, Washington; p. 31 (tr): Douglas
Peebles/CORBIS/Magma; p. 36 (br): William A. Bake/CORBIS/Magma; p. 38 (tr): Kevin
Schafer/CORBIS/Magma; p. 38 (br): EQE International, Inc.; p. 54 (bl): Ocean Remote
Sensing Group, Johns Hopkins University, Applied Physics Laboratory; p. 57 (tl): Rick
Doyle/CORBIS/Magma; p. 60 (cl & bl): Scott Walking Adventure

Printed in Canada

1 2 3 4 5 6 7 8 9 05 04 03 02 01

Table of Contents

4 | Earth's History

6 The Formation of Earth

8 The Geologic Time Scale

10 Life Emerges on the Continents

12 | Earth's Structure

14 Inside Earth

16 The Minerals

18 The Life Cycle of Rocks

20 Types of Rocks

22 | Tectonics and Volcanism

24 Plate Tectonics

26 The Fate of Pangaea

28 Continental Drift

30 Volcanoes

32 Volcanism

34 Volcanic Eruptions

35 Hot Spots

36 Geysers

38 Earthquakes

40 Seismic Waves

42 | Water and Oceans

44 Watercourses

46 The World's Rivers and Lakes

48 The World Ocean

50 The Ocean Floor

52 Oceanic Trenches and Ridges

54 Ocean Currents

56 Waves

58 Tsunamis

60 The Tides

62 Glossary

63 Books

63 Videos

63 Web Sites

64 Index

Earth, formed 4.6 billion years ago from a cloud of dust, did not always look like the planet that we know today. In fact, it has been changing constantly throughout its history, becoming increasingly organized and complex. This fascinating evolution is revealed through the rocks and fossils that provide evidence of our planet's early times.

Earth's History

6   **The Formation of Earth**
How it all got started

8   **The Geologic Time Scale**
Finding the origins of life

10 **Life Emerges on the Continents**
Increasingly complex organisms

The Formation of Earth

How it all got started

Five billion years ago, the Solar System did not exist. There was only a huge, diffuse cloud of dust and gases turning slowly on itself. Over time, the Sun was formed, followed by the nine planets, including Earth, which formed a bit like a snowball, by the agglomeration of matter around the original nebula.

EMERGING FROM A CLOUD OF DUST

It all started 4.6 billion years ago, in one of the spiral arms of the Milky Way. Impacted by a shock wave that probably came from the explosion of massive stars, a cloud of dust (the **solar nebula**) began to rotate ❶.

At the center of the cloud, matter became increasingly dense, hot, and luminous. It gave rise to an embryonic star, which became the **Sun** ❷.

Dust in the surrounding area began to agglomerate. Small pebbles grew larger, forming embryonic planets, or **protoplanets**, a few miles (a few kilometers) in diameter ❸.

The protoplanets collided with each other and agglomerated until they reached the size of **planets** several thousand miles (several thousand km) in diameter. Over hundreds of millions of years, the emerging planets were intensely bombarded by other rocky bodies ❹.

LIFE ARISES FROM A BALL OF LAVA

When it was first formed, about 4.6 billion years ago, Earth was completely covered with an **ocean of burning lava** (liquid rock) several hundred miles (several hundred km) thick. It had neither crust nor core ❺.

Little by little, the ocean of lava cooled. **Pieces of crust** formed and floated on the surface of the planet, which was being intensely bombarded by meteorites and comets ❻.

Over time, an **early crust** formed. The heavy elements, such as iron and nickel, concentrated to form the core, while the lighter elements (including oxygen, silicon, and aluminum) formed the crust ❼.

Earth was also host to intense volcanic activity, which led to the expulsion of light gases and liberated an **early atmosphere** that was radically different from today's. As it condensed, water vapor formed clouds; the advent of rain enabled lakes, rivers, and oceans to be created. At the same time, the crust broke up and formed continents ❽.

The presence of continents, oceans, and an oxygen-poor atmosphere resulted in the formation of more and more complex molecules, which led to a remarkable phenomenon: **life**. More than a billion years after Earth was formed, life appeared in the oceans ❾. It then took a few billion years to emerge onto the continents!

meteorite

volcano

crater

continent

ocean

❺

❻

❼

8

❾

The Geologic Time Scale

Finding the origins of life

Since it came into being, 4.6 billion years ago, Earth has undergone numerous transformations. At the beginning, it bore absolutely no resemblance to what we see today. The planet's landscape changed very slowly: continents and oceans formed, animal and plant species appeared and then were replaced by others.

To determine and date the major transformations of a world in perpetual change, geologists have created a geologic time scale.

THE BEGINNINGS OF THE WORLD: AQUATIC LIFE

The Precambrian ❶ is the oldest and longest period in the history of Earth. During this time, 4 billion years ago, the terrestrial crust was formed, followed by the continents and oceans. Life came into being 500 million years later, when the first cellular organisms appeared, along with the first bacteria and algae.

In the Cambrian Period ❷, various groups of invertebrates evolved in the shallow seas that covered much of Earth.

The first vertebrates appeared in the following period, the Ordovician ❸. There were also great quantities of coral, sponges, and mollusks such as cephalopods.

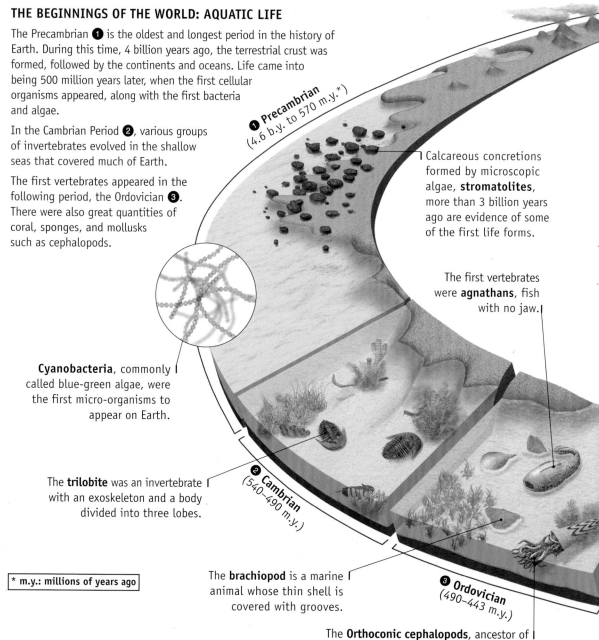

❶ **Precambrian** (4.6 b.y. to 570 m.y.*)

Calcareous concretions formed by microscopic algae, **stromatolites**, more than 3 billion years ago are evidence of some of the first life forms.

The first vertebrates were **agnathans**, fish with no jaw.

Cyanobacteria, commonly called blue-green algae, were the first micro-organisms to appear on Earth.

The **trilobite** was an invertebrate with an exoskeleton and a body divided into three lobes.

❷ **Cambrian** (540–490 m.y.)

The **brachiopod** is a marine animal whose thin shell is covered with grooves.

❸ **Ordovician** (490–443 m.y.)

The **Orthoconic cephalopods**, ancestor of the squid, the octopus, and the *Nautilus*, had a straight or slightly curved shell.

* m.y.: millions of years ago

THE HISTORY OF EARTH IN ONE YEAR

It's difficult to conceive of such a huge stretch of time as 4.6 billion years of evolution, but we can get an idea by squeezing the period into one year. Imagine that Earth was created at midnight on January 1. The first life form appeared in April. Plants started to grow on land at the end of November. Dinosaurs walked the Earth in mid-December and disappeared on December 25 at around 7:00 P.M. Human beings populated Earth on December 31 at 11:25 P.M. and built the pyramids in Egypt at 11:59.29 P.M. Europeans first arrived in America at 11:59.57 P.M.!

THE CONQUEST OF EARTH

During the Silurian Period ❹, the first land-based plants grew, and fish with jaws began to appear.

The Devonian Period ❺ marked the arrival of insects and the first land-based animals: amphibians. During this period, fish species became more diversified, and the continents, previously barren, began to be covered with horsetails and ferns.

During the Carboniferous Period ❻, a rise in sea levels led to the formation of huge marshes. Dead vegetation accumulated, forming layers of peat that became deposits of coal. The first reptiles appeared.

Ferns began to grow on the water's edge. Some were small, but others were as tall as today's trees.

The oldest insect known, the **Archaeognath**, had no wings, but it did have long antennae.

Over time, the fins of some fish were transformed into limbs. The **Ichthyostega** was one of the first amphibians to evolve. Its tail looked like a fishtail.

Acanthodians, the first fish with jaws, appeared during the Silurian Period. Their fins had long spines.

Cooksonia were among the first plants to grow on land. They consisted of stems, with no leaves or roots.

The oldest winged insects date from this period. Among them was the **giant dragonfly, Meganeura**, with a wingspan of 27 inches (70 centimeters).

In coniferous forests, millipedes such as the **Arthropleura** measured up to 6.5 feet (2 meters) in length.

Sharks were among the dominant fish of the Carboniferous Period. Some genera, such as the **Falcatus**, had a jagged spine on top of their heads.

❹ **Silurian**
(443–417 m.y.)

❺ **Devonian**
(417–354 m.y.)

❻ **Carboniferous**
(354–290 m.y.)

Life Emerges on the Continents

Increasingly complex organisms

REPTILES, MAMMALS, AND DINOSAURS

In the Permian Period ❼, reptiles abounded, taking over from amphibians as the climate became drier. At this time, the continental masses formed a single supercontinent: Pangaea.

During the Triassic Period ❽, the supercontinent began to break up, giving rise to today's continents. Mammals, dinosaurs, and a variety of aquatic reptiles appeared.

During the following period, the Jurassic ❾, Pangaea broke apart, creating a space that became the Atlantic Ocean. Dinosaurs such as *Diplodocus* and *Apatosaurus* dominated the planet. Some reptiles and the first birds·took flight. Flowering plants began to grow.

Dimetrodon was one of the carnivorous reptiles that dominated the Permian Period. This animal's large sail enabled it to regulate its body temperature.

Diplodocus was one of the largest dinosaurs of the Jurassic Period. This long-necked herbivore may have stood on its hind legs to reach the leaves on trees.

Archaeopteryx, one of the earliest winged animals, had features typical of both reptiles (claws, teeth, long tail) and birds (wings, feathers).

Among the Triassic Period dinosaurs was the **biped** *Coelophysis*, a voracious predator with powerful talons.

The mouse-sized *Megazostrodon* was one of the first mammals to appear on Earth. An insectivore, it was active mainly at night.

❼ **Permian** (286–245 m.y.*)

The first marine reptile, the *Mesosaurus*, was a small animal that had a long, pointed muzzle and swam in shallow waters.

❽ **Triassic** (245-208 m.y.)

A medium-sized, long-necked reptile, the *Nothosaurus* had webbed feet adapted for swimming.

❾ **Jurassic** (208-145 m.y.)

The *Ichthyosaurus* looked similar to a dolphin. This marine reptile measured from 3 to 16 feet (1 to 5 m) in length and was very well adapted to aquatic life.

THE ARRIVAL OF HUMAN BEINGS

The dinosaurs, which ruled Earth for part of the Triassic Period and the entire Jurassic and Cretaceous periods ❿, suddenly disappeared at the end of the Cretaceous Period, probably following a collision of Earth with a giant meteorite that caused the extinction of three-fourths of all animal and plant species.

The first primates and great apes appeared during the Tertiary Period ⓫. As mammal species began to diversify, horses, camels, rhinoceroses, and elephants evolved. A climatic cooling led to the formation of prairies.

The Quaternary Period ⓬ was punctuated by four ice ages: glaciers reached their maximum advance eighteen thousand years ago and withdrew eight thousand years later. During this period, mammals and birds were the dominant species and the first hominids appeared. Historical time began with the invention of writing, five thousand years ago.

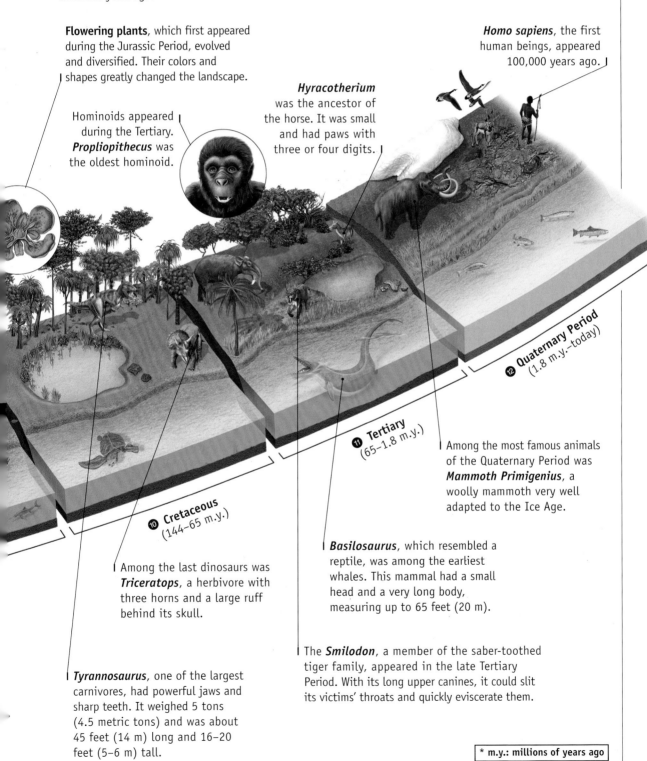

Flowering plants, which first appeared during the Jurassic Period, evolved and diversified. Their colors and shapes greatly changed the landscape.

Hominoids appeared during the Tertiary. **Propliopithecus** was the oldest hominoid.

Hyracotherium was the ancestor of the horse. It was small and had paws with three or four digits.

Homo sapiens, the first human beings, appeared 100,000 years ago.

❿ **Cretaceous** (144–65 m.y.)

⓫ **Tertiary** (65–1.8 m.y.)

⓬ **Quaternary Period** (1.8 m.y.–today)

Among the last dinosaurs was **Triceratops**, a herbivore with three horns and a large ruff behind its skull.

Basilosaurus, which resembled a reptile, was among the earliest whales. This mammal had a small head and a very long body, measuring up to 65 feet (20 m).

Among the most famous animals of the Quaternary Period was **Mammoth Primigenius**, a woolly mammoth very well adapted to the Ice Age.

Tyrannosaurus, one of the largest carnivores, had powerful jaws and sharp teeth. It weighed 5 tons (4.5 metric tons) and was about 45 feet (14 m) long and 16–20 feet (5–6 m) tall.

The **Smilodon**, a member of the saber-toothed tiger family, appeared in the late Tertiary Period. With its long upper canines, it could slit its victims' throats and quickly eviscerate them.

* m.y.: millions of years ago

What is under Earth's surface? Can we reach the planet's core? The inside of Earth, with its extreme pressures and temperatures, is still a mysterious place. In a process that has been going on for billions of years, minerals are formed there and then metamorphosed into many shapes and stunning structures.

Earth's Structure

14 **Inside Earth**
The planet's internal structure

16 **The Minerals**
The crystalline core of rocks

18 **The Life Cycle of Rocks**
Earth's materials in constant evolution

20 **Types of Rocks**
An extraordinary diversity

Inside Earth

The planet's internal structure

Although we cannot know exactly what the internal structure of our planet looks like, geophysics and astronomy (by observation and analysis of other planets in the Solar System) have enabled us to gather much information concerning the inside of Earth.

Our planet has a total mass of about 6 billion billion tons and is made of three concentric layers — the core, the mantle, and the crust (from the densest to the lightest) — edged by transition zones called discontinuities. Each layer has its own chemical composition and physical properties.

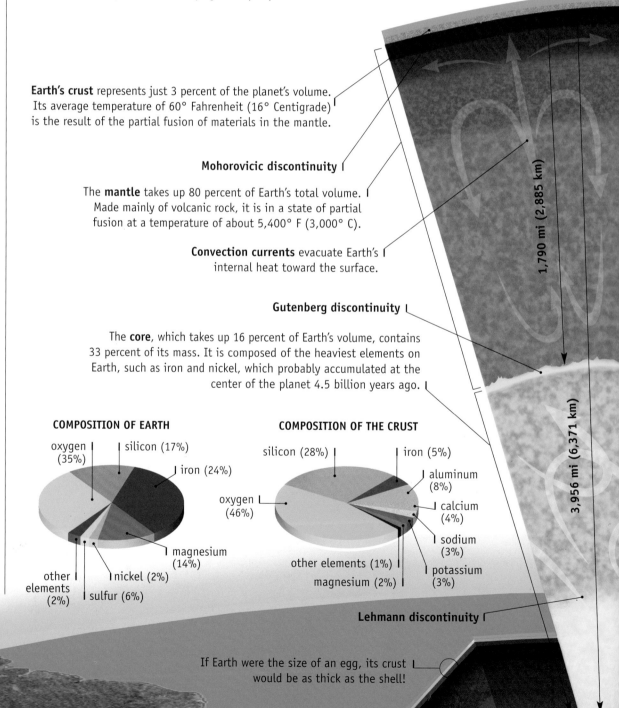

Earth's crust represents just 3 percent of the planet's volume. Its average temperature of 60° Fahrenheit (16° Centigrade) is the result of the partial fusion of materials in the mantle.

Mohorovicic discontinuity

The **mantle** takes up 80 percent of Earth's total volume. Made mainly of volcanic rock, it is in a state of partial fusion at a temperature of about 5,400° F (3,000° C).

Convection currents evacuate Earth's internal heat toward the surface.

Gutenberg discontinuity

The **core**, which takes up 16 percent of Earth's volume, contains 33 percent of its mass. It is composed of the heaviest elements on Earth, such as iron and nickel, which probably accumulated at the center of the planet 4.5 billion years ago.

1,790 mi (2,885 km)

3,956 mi (6,371 km)

COMPOSITION OF EARTH

oxygen (35%)
silicon (17%)
iron (24%)
magnesium (14%)
nickel (2%)
sulfur (6%)
other elements (2%)

COMPOSITION OF THE CRUST

silicon (28%)
iron (5%)
aluminum (8%)
calcium (4%)
sodium (3%)
potassium (3%)
magnesium (2%)
other elements (1%)
oxygen (46%)

Lehmann discontinuity

If Earth were the size of an egg, its crust would be as thick as the shell!

Most of Earth's surface consists of an **oceanic crust** that is quite thin — about 6 miles (10 km) thick.

The **continental crust** is thicker than the oceanic crust, at 19 to 25 miles (30 to 40 km) thick and up to 43 miles (70 km) under mountain belts.

The rigid outer shell of Earth, the **lithosphere**, is formed of the crust and the top of the upper mantle.

In the **asthenosphere**, the temperature is above 2200° F (1200° C) and rocks melt. The plasticity of this layer allows continental drift to occur.

The **top of the upper mantle** is a rigid layer lying just below the crust.

The **upper mantle** is composed of hard rocks, which are rich in iron and magnesium-bearing silicates, and the asthenosphere, which is capable of flowing.

The **lower mantle** occurs just below the asthenosphere. Little is known about this zone, but it is formed of liquid materials that are moved by slow convection currents.

DEPTHS BEYOND SOUNDING

Our knowledge of Earth's structures is based on indirect observation, especially the study of seismic waves. No drilling has ever penetrated farther into the ground than 9.3 miles (15 km), which corresponds only to the superficial part of the crust.

The **outer core**, composed of metals in a fluid state, is what gives rise to Earth's magnetic field.

The **inner core** is made up of metal in a solid state, even though the temperature is above 10,800 °F (6,000 °C). This is probably due to the extreme pressure.

mining operation
2.6 mi (3.8 km)

undersea exploration
6.5 mi (10.5 km)

geologic exploration
9.3 mi (15 km)

The Minerals

The crystalline core of rocks

Earth's crust is composed of rocks and minerals. There are about 3,500 minerals, each of which is unique. Minerals can be classified according to specific characteristics: color, streak, transparency, hardness, crystalline structure, and facies or texture are among the many features that are used to group them by family. Some minerals are not abundant, and some are very rare. Some, such as diamond, are considered precious. Others, such as agate, are not precious, but because of their shape or color they are considered gems, which are minerals used in jewelry.

ROCK OR MINERAL?

Rocks and minerals are often confused. In fact, rocks are aggregates of several minerals. Granite, for example, is made of quartz, feldspar, and mica.

Minerals are inorganic solid bodies, produced naturally, that have a defined chemical composition and atomic structure.

quartz

feldspar

granite

mica

CHEMICAL BONDS AND AGGLOMERATION

The combination of chemical elements ❶ constitutes the starting point for the formation of minerals. They form a basic molecular structure called unit cells ❷, which bond with other cells to form a solid with a well-defined structure: a crystal ❸. Subjected to underground pressure, the various crystals agglomerate ❹ to produce the rocks ❺ found in the subsoil ❻.

❶   ❷   ❸   ❹   ❺   ❻

THE COMPOSITION OF MINERALS

Minerals are usually classified into twelve families according to their chemical composition. Some of them, such as native elements whose main characteristic is that they are formed of a single chemical element, are better known than others. Metals, such as gold and silver, are in this family. Diamond and graphite are also native elements; both are composed of carbon atoms, even though their color, transparency, and hardness are different.

gold   silver   diamond   graphite

COLOR

Minerals can be identified by color. Some minerals, such as malachite, are always the same color. Others, such as fluorite and quartz, are found in various shades depending on the kinds of impurities present in the crystal. They are called allochromatic.

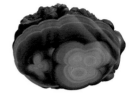

malachite

purple, yellow, and green fluorite

pink and white quartz

STREAK

A streak is the line of powder that a mineral leaves on a surface of unpolished porcelain. Minerals with the same crystalline structure always leave a streak of the same color.

The steak of **crocoite** is orangey-yellow.

Although **chalcopyrite** is gold in color, its streak is always a greenish black.

Cinnabar leaves a red streak.

Orpiment leaves a golden-yellow streak.

TRANSPARENCY

The amount of light that a mineral lets pass through attests to its transparency, translucency, or opacity.

If we can see an object through a mineral, it is **transparent**. Quartz is such a mineral.

If only light passes through it, the mineral is **translucent**. Agate has this characteristic.

An opaque mineral lets no light pass through it. Copper is a good example.

THE MOHS SCALE

The Mohs scale compares the hardness of minerals on a scale of 1 to 10, from the softest (1) to the hardest (10). Each mineral is classified according to how it scratches the others or is scratched by them. For example, talc, which can be scratched by a fingernail, has a hardness of 1, while calcite, which can be scratched by a coin, has a hardness of 3. Quartz, which can scratch glass, has a hardness of 7. Diamond, the hardest mineral, cannot be scratched, and thus it has the highest rating.

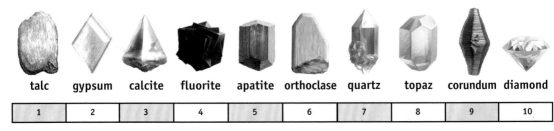

talc	gypsum	calcite	fluorite	apatite	orthoclase	quartz	topaz	corundum	diamond
1	2	3	4	5	6	7	8	9	10

The Life Cycle of Rocks

Earth's materials in constant evolution

People often say that something is hard as a rock, meaning that it will never change. But contrary to popular belief, rocks are constantly changing. They are continually being formed, deformed, and transformed, sinking from the surface of Earth to its depths, then re-emerging.

Rocks are recycled by nature and subjected to a variety of chemical and physical processes that last millions of years. There are three types of rocks: sedimentary, metamorphic, and igneous.

SEDIMENTATION

Broken up by various climatic phenomena such as the wind and rain ❶ or worn away by erosion ❷, rocks gradually crumble into small particles. These particles are transported by watercourses ❸, then deposited to form sedimentary rocks ❹, which may sink into the mantle ❺. Movements of Earth's crust may also carry rocks deeper ❻. Some sedimentary rocks will be brought back to the surface more rapidly ❼.

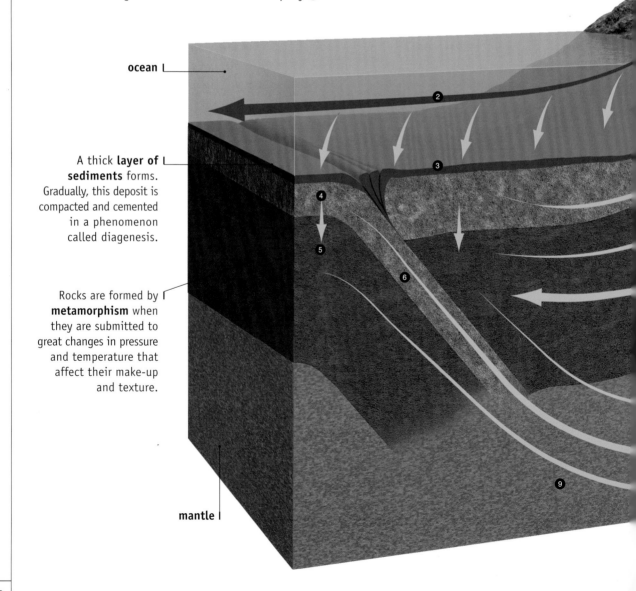

ocean

A thick **layer of sediments** forms. Gradually, this deposit is compacted and cemented in a phenomenon called diagenesis.

Rocks are formed by **metamorphism** when they are submitted to great changes in pressure and temperature that affect their make-up and texture.

mantle

METAMORPHISM AND MAGMATISM

When rocks are subjected to high pressure and temperatures, they undergo major metamorphoses. Some metamorphic rocks rise directly to the surface ❽, while others sink deeper into the mantle ❾, where they melt and are transformed into magma ❿. When magma rises in Earth's crust ⓫, it sometimes solidifies before reaching the surface, forming plutonic igneous rocks. These rocks may undergo further metamorphoses ⓬. On the other hand, volcanic igneous rocks remain in a liquid state (lava) until they are erupted ⓭ and solidify on Earth's surface.

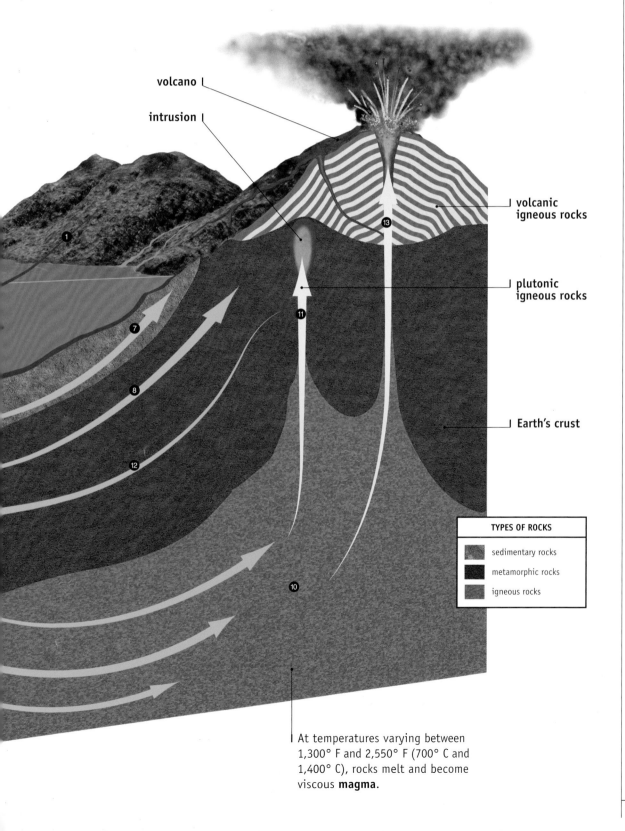

volcano

intrusion

volcanic igneous rocks

plutonic igneous rocks

Earth's crust

TYPES OF ROCKS

sedimentary rocks

metamorphic rocks

igneous rocks

At temperatures varying between 1,300° F and 2,550° F (700° C and 1,400° C), rocks melt and become viscous **magma**.

Types of Rocks

An extraordinary diversity

Rocks are defined as assemblages of minerals: they are solids composed of an immense variety of combinations of chemical elements, all of which are well known today. This huge group is divided into three general categories: sedimentary, metamorphic, and igneous rocks.

SEDIMENTARY ROCKS

Sedimentary rocks form at the surface of Earth or in bodies of water. Far from being composed only of mineral elements, they also contain animal and plant debris that have become bonded to mineral particles. There are three types of sedimentary rocks: biogenic rocks, formed of organic debris; detrital rocks, formed of various types of debris; and rocks of chemical origin.

Rock salt is a chemical rock and one of the evaporites: it is formed by precipitation when seawater evaporates and leaves a salt deposit.

Formed by the agglomeration of grains of sand, **sandstone** is a detrital rock that is often used in construction.

Chalk, made mainly of calcite, is a very fine-grained rock with a friable and porous texture. It is a biogenic rock formed of marine microfossils.

Coal is a biogenic rock formed of plant debris. It forms in shallow water, such as marshes. Also known as charcoal, it is used as a fuel.

Limestone is a biogenic rock that contains shell debris. Fossiliferous limestone contains fossils.

METAMORPHIC ROCKS

Metamorphic rocks are rocks that have been exposed to such intense pressure or temperature that their structure has been altered. Under these conditions, they do not melt but crystallize, and they have a foliated or banded texture.

Quartzite results from the metamorphosis of siliceous sandstone. It is composed of aggregated quartz.

Granite gneiss is a foliated rock that results from the deformation of granite. It is composed of thin light- and dark-colored layers.

Under heat or pressure, limestone is transformed into **marble**. This veined rock, in various colors, has been prized by architects and sculptors for centuries. Carrare marble from Italy is among the most famous.

Pressure and heat transform shale into **slate**. This black, green, or grey rock flakes easily; it has long been used for roofs and blackboards.

| mantle

IGNEOUS ROCKS

Igneous rocks generally come from Earth's upper mantle, where magma is partially melted. Depending on their rate of cooling, these rocks will be more or less fine grained. Plutonic (or intrusive) rocks, which solidify slowly, are coarse-grained, while volcanic (extrusive) rocks, which solidify rapidly when they reach the surface, are fine-grained.

Basalt is the most common volcanic rock. Resulting from the solidification of lava, it is dark colored, usually black or very dark green. A number of volcanic islands, including those of Hawaii, are made mainly of basalt.

Made essentially of quartz, feldspar, and mica, **granite** is the best-known plutonic rock. Granites are very often used in the construction of monuments and buildings.

Although it seems immobile, the ground we stand on moves several inches (several cm) every year. The huge plates that form Earth's crust drift on the surface of the planet and collide with each other, imperceptibly building mountains and hollowing out ocean beds. In fact, these slow yet continuous movements are responsible for the most sudden and devastating phenomena on the planet: volcanic eruptions and earthquakes.

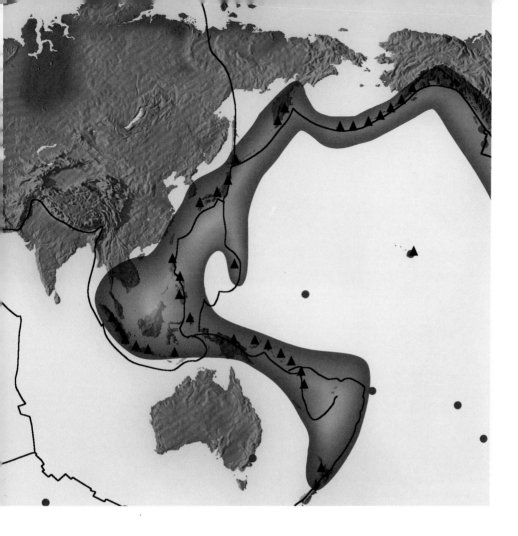

Tectonics and Volcanism

24 **Plate Tectonics**
Earth's surface in motion

26 **The Fate of Pangaea**
The break-up of a supercontinent

28 **Continental Drift**
Earth, from the past to the future

30 **Volcanoes**
Astonishing mountains

32 **Volcanism**
A rumbling threat all over the world

34 **Volcanic Eruptions**
When mountaintops explode

35 **Hot Spots**
Volcanoes in a row

36 **Geysers**
When Earth spits up water

38 **Earthquakes**
A sudden liberation of energy

40 **Seismic Waves**
Measuring and locating earthquakes

Plate Tectonics

Earth's surface in motion

The ground on which we stand is much less still than it appears: each year, Europe and North America move apart from each other by an inch (2.5 cm), while India and Asia move 2 to 3 inches (4 to 6 cm) closer; some parts of the world move 7 inches (18 cm). This phenomenon is called plate tectonics. It results from the fact that the lithosphere (the outer layer of Earth) is broken into thirteen plates (huge solid surfaces about 60 miles [100 km] thick) that slide on the asthenosphere, part of Earth's upper mantle.

CONVERGING, DIVERGING AND TRANSFORM PLATES

Plate tectonics accounts for most of the relief features on Earth's surface, from oceans, created when two plates move apart from each other, to mountain ranges, which are formed when two plates collide. The way that the plates meet is the deciding factor. Converging plates may collide or slide under one another (this is called subduction); diverging plates move away from each other, causing magma to rise and generate new crust; transform (or strike-slip) plates slide past each other.

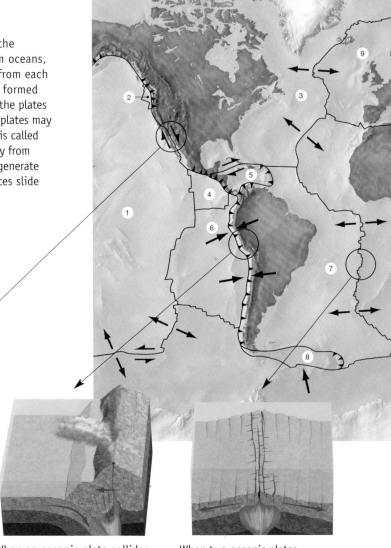

Transform plates slide by each other without converging or diverging. When they do so, they often cause earthquakes. This is the case for the **San Andreas Fault**, off the coast of California, where the Pacific and North American plates meet.

When an oceanic plate collides with a continental plate, the oceanic plate slides underneath because it is denser. Where this occurs, volcanic mountain ranges rise at the edge of the continent. The **Andes Cordillera** was formed this way.

When two oceanic plates move apart, a divergence zone is created, causing magma to rise. Volcanic mountains are formed in this zone from the rise of magma. The **mid-Atlantic ridge** is one of the submarine mountain belts known as oceanic ridges.

CONVECTION CURRENTS

As it rises, Earth's internal heat causes convection movements, or currents, that cause the tectonic plates to move. These currents form a sort of giant conveyor belt on which old crust gives way to new. Lava ❶ that flows from the ridges ❷ opens a fissure ❸ through which magma will cool and form new oceanic crust ❹. Because Earth stays the same size, there are subduction zones ❺ where old crust is folded under and consumed by the magma ❻.

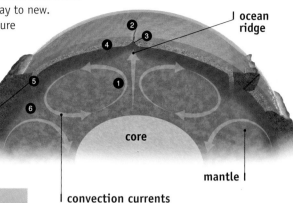

ocean ridge

subduction zone

core

mantle

convection currents

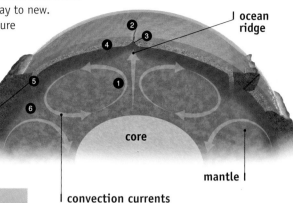

converging plates
diverging plates
transform plates
subduction

A PLANET IN PIECES

Thirteen main tectonic plates exist, with widely varying areas. Some plates support both oceans and continents; others, only one or the other (these are either oceanic or continental plates).

1. Pacific Plate
2. Juan de Fuca Plate
3. North American Plate
4. Cocos Plate
5. Caribbean Plate
6. Nazca Plate
7. South American Plate

8. Scotia Plate
9. Eurasian Plate
10. African Plate
11. Antarctic Plate
12. Indian-Australian Plate
13. Philippine Sea Plate

Like the oceanic plates, the continental plates may move apart. This is the case for the **East African Great Rift Valley**, a large subsidence zone the lowest parts of which are gradually being invaded by the sea.

When two continental plates converge, they sometimes stick together. Under the effect of compression, the crust gets thicker and folds. The **Himalayas** in the high plateau of Tibet are evidence of such a collision.

When two oceanic plates converge, the denser plate slides beneath the other one. Magma rises to form island arcs, such as the **Philippine Archipelago**.

The Fate of Pangaea

The break-up of a supercontinent

In the early twentieth century, Alfred Wegener, a German climatologist and geophysicist, noted that continents seemed to be able to fit together. He observed, for example, that the contours of western Africa matched those of South America almost perfectly and that similar geologic formations existed on both continents.

This observation gave rise to the hypothesis that there was a single huge continent millions of years ago, but it was not until the 1960s that Wegener's intuitions were confirmed and accepted. Today, it is agreed that a supercontinent called Pangaea (meaning "all the land") was surrounded by a single ocean, Panthalassa ("all the oceans"). It gradually broke apart, creating new continents and new oceans, and the continents are still drifting.

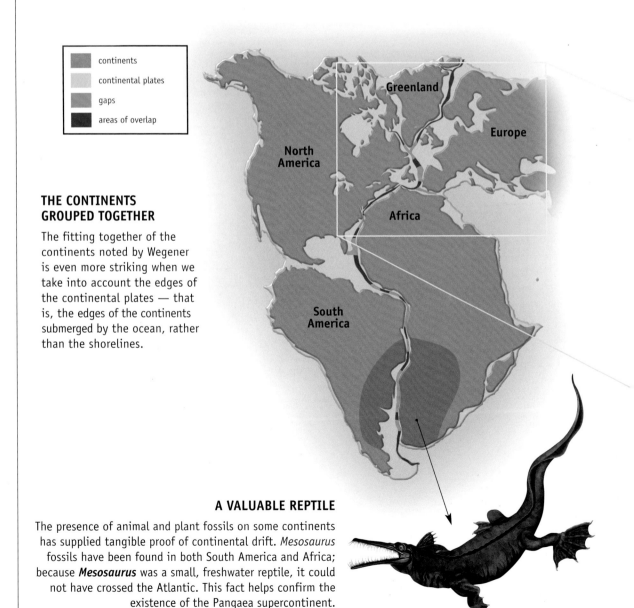

	continents
	continental plates
	gaps
	areas of overlap

Greenland

Europe

North America

Africa

South America

THE CONTINENTS GROUPED TOGETHER

The fitting together of the continents noted by Wegener is even more striking when we take into account the edges of the continental plates — that is, the edges of the continents submerged by the ocean, rather than the shorelines.

A VALUABLE REPTILE

The presence of animal and plant fossils on some continents has supplied tangible proof of continental drift. *Mesosaurus* fossils have been found in both South America and Africa; because **Mesosaurus** was a small, freshwater reptile, it could not have crossed the Atlantic. This fact helps confirm the existence of the Pangaea supercontinent.

ICE IN THE TROPICS?

Among the other facts that support the theory of continental drift is the presence of glacial deposits in the southern regions of some continents. Traces of glaciation can be found in South America, Australia, and even Africa and India, areas that are now decidedly tropical. These glacial deposits, which indicate that ice flowed toward the interior of continents, were probably left by glaciers hundreds of millions of years ago.

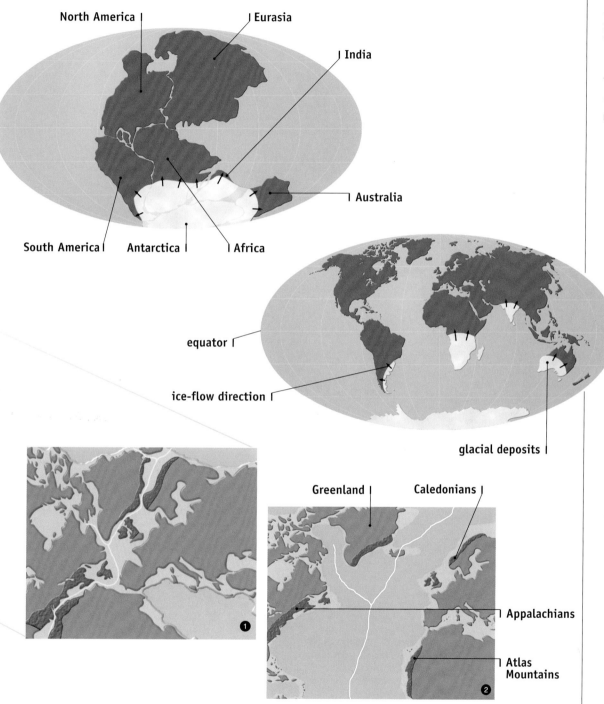

CONCORDANT MOUNTAINS

One of the decisive arguments in favor of continental drift is the striking similarity between geological structures in different parts of the world. If we visualize North America, Europe, and Africa side by side, we see an important mountain belt emerge ❶. Incidentally, the three mountain ranges that we find today on either side of the Atlantic — the Appalachians, the Caledonians, and the Atlas Mountains — are the same age (about 300 million years old) and have identical geologic structures ❷.

Continental Drift

Earth, from the past to the future

In the 1960s, Wegener's ideas concerning continental drift were supported by new discoveries. The spread of ocean floors and plate tectonics explain the movement of Earth's surface and the mechanism of continental drift. Thanks to convection currents within Earth, the plates that carry the continents slide over the asthenosphere, the viscous layer of the planet. The currents carry the plates toward or away from each other at a speed of between .4 and 7 inches (between 1 and 18 cm) per year. The spread of ocean floors still pushes continents apart even more when new divergent zones develop under them. Thus, the movement of continents continues today.

EARTH 200 MILLION YEARS AGO

Masses of land moved together to form a supercontinent, Pangaea, with the Panthalassa to the west and the Tethys Sea to the east.

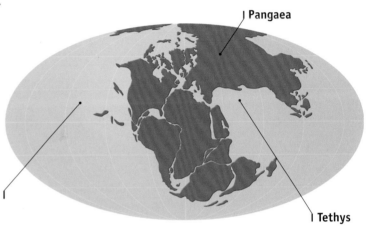

Pangaea

Panthalassa

Tethys

EARTH 150 MILLION YEARS AGO

Two of the masses separate, creating the continent Laurasia to the north (today's North America and Eurasia) and the continent Gondwana to the south (today's South America, Africa, Australia, and India). The Indian Ocean gradually opens. Pangaea no longer exists.

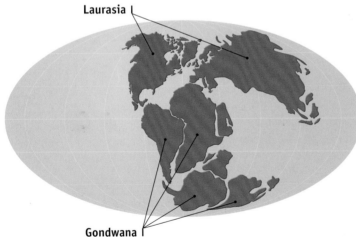

Laurasia

Gondwana

EARTH 100 MILLION YEARS AGO

Australia and Antarctica separate. A fault splits Gondwana, and South America separates from Africa. As the continental masses move away, the waters of the Tethys Sea infiltrate the fault. The Atlantic Ocean takes shape.

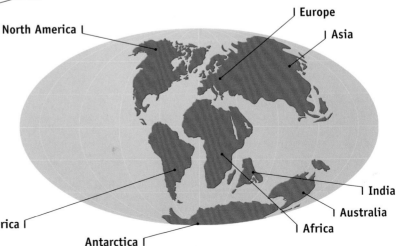

Europe

Asia

North America

India

Australia

Africa

South America

Antarctica

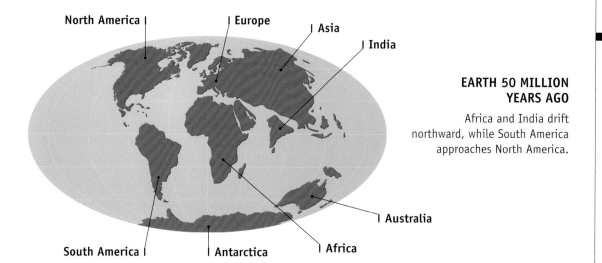

EARTH 50 MILLION YEARS AGO

Africa and India drift northward, while South America approaches North America.

North America | Europe | Asia | India | Australia | Africa | Antarctica | South America

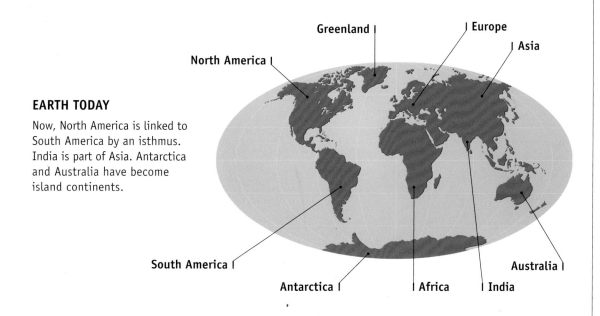

EARTH TODAY

Now, North America is linked to South America by an isthmus. India is part of Asia. Antarctica and Australia have become island continents.

Greenland | Europe | Asia | North America | South America | Antarctica | Africa | India | Australia

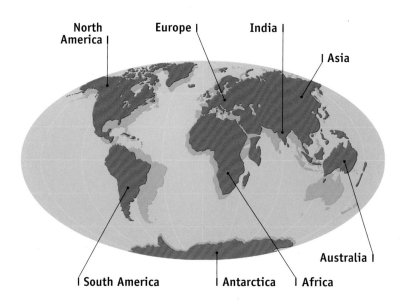

EARTH IN 50 MILLION YEARS

The northward drift of West Africa toward the Mediterranean Sea will compress Corsica, Sardinia, and Sicily and close off the warm sea while creating an impressive mountain belt. Arabia and Africa will separate, making the Red Sea into a new ocean. Australia will drift toward Asia, while India will continue moving into that continent, further raising the Himalayan mountain range.

North America | Europe | India | Asia | South America | Antarctica | Africa | Australia

Volcanoes

Astonishing mountains

Volcanic eruptions are among the most spectacular observable natural phenomena. They are evidence of Earth's activity and show that volcanoes are not ordinary mountains.

Since our planet was formed, volcanic activity has probably contributed to the development of the oceans and to life on Earth through the emission of gases, steam, and materials from the planet's depths. Nevertheless, volcanoes are most often associated with their destructive power and the catastrophes they cause.

THE PHENOMENON OF VOLCANOES

As it rises toward the surface, hot, light magma ❶ (molten rock) from Earth's mantle is stored in the magma chamber ❷. Over time, the accumulation of material pushes the magma into the vent ❸ and brings it to the surface, where it is ejected from the crater ❹. Molten lava flows ❺ down the sides of the volcanic structure. The eruptive column ❻ is made up of gas and rocks of various sizes that are ejected from the crater. The magma that doesn't reach the surface sometimes penetrates into a layer of a different type of rock and solidifies ❼ to form dykes, laccoliths, or sills. This phenomenon is called intrusion.

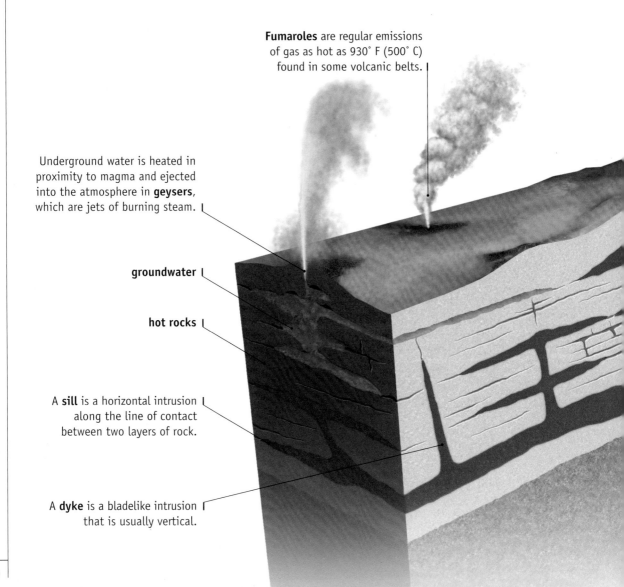

Fumaroles are regular emissions of gas as hot as 930° F (500° C) found in some volcanic belts.

Underground water is heated in proximity to magma and ejected into the atmosphere in **geysers**, which are jets of burning steam.

groundwater

hot rocks

A **sill** is a horizontal intrusion along the line of contact between two layers of rock.

A **dyke** is a bladelike intrusion that is usually vertical.

TYPES OF ERUPTIONS

In June 1991, Mount **Pinatubo**, in the Philippines, erupted after more than six centuries of dormancy. The pressure caused the volcano's dome to be pulverized, and debris was violently ejected.

The **Kilauea** volcano, on the island of Hawaii, is among the best-known active volcanoes. Since 1983, this effusive-type volcano has been discharging long rivers of boiling lava.

Particles of **ash** measuring less than .08 inch (2 mm) are made of pulverized magma or crushed rock.

Lapilli are tiny stones, measuring .04 to 2.5 inches (1 to 64 mm), ejected in a solid or semi-solid state.

Pieces of magma measuring more than 2.5 inches (64 mm) and projected very high are called **volcanic bombs.**

Lava, with a temperature of more than 1,800° F (1,000° C), flows at an average speed of 975 feet (300 m) per hour.

The **deposits** of ash and lava from successive eruptions form a series of layers that eventually becomes a volcanic cone.

A **laccolith** is an intrusion with a horizontal base and a dome-shaped top.

Volcanism

A rumbling threat all over the world

In certain regions scattered all over the world, volcanoes can spring to life, sometimes after thousands of years of dormancy, and erupt violently. Although some eruptions are short, others are long and dangerous. Some last almost ten years! The clouds of ash that escape into the atmosphere can take months, or even a year, to dissipate.

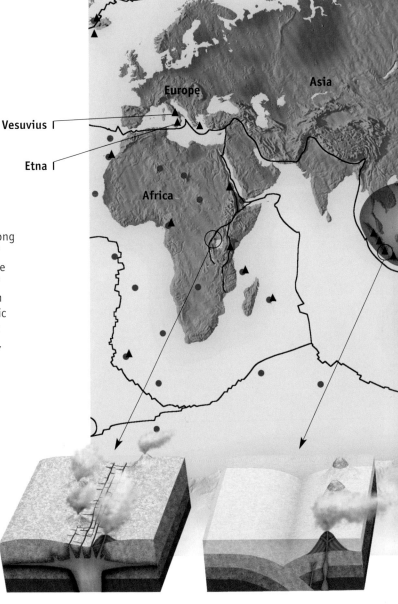

THE RING OF FIRE

Most volcanoes emerge in chains along the edges of tectonic plates. One of the best-known volcanic regions is the Ring of Fire, which contains many of the world's volcanoes. Arranged in an island arc stretching around the Pacific Ocean, the ring includes the volcanic archipelagos of the Aleutians, Japan, and the Philippines.

TYPES OF VOLCANISM

There are three types of volcanism, and each may appear on continents or in the oceans. The first two types are directly linked to the phenomenon of tectonic plates: subduction volcanism (plate convergence) and fissure volcanism (divergence). The third type occurs not at the edges of two plates but within a single plate: intraplate volcanism, also known as hot spots.

Spreading continental plates cause **fissure volcanism**. The East African Great Rift Valley is forming along one of these faults located on the African continent.

Oceanic subduction volcanism occurs when one plate slides under another. The infiltration of water into the depths of Earth causes a lowering of pressure that encourages magma to rise, leading to particularly explosive eruptions. Krakatoa is this type of volcano.

GEOGRAPHIC DISTRIBUTION

A volcano is considered active if it erupts at least once every one hundred years. It is estimated that there are fifteen hundred active volcanoes on the continents, with about fifty eruptions each year; more are on the ocean bottom. The geographic distribution of volcanoes is not haphazard; it corresponds to hot spots and to fracture zones along plate boundaries.

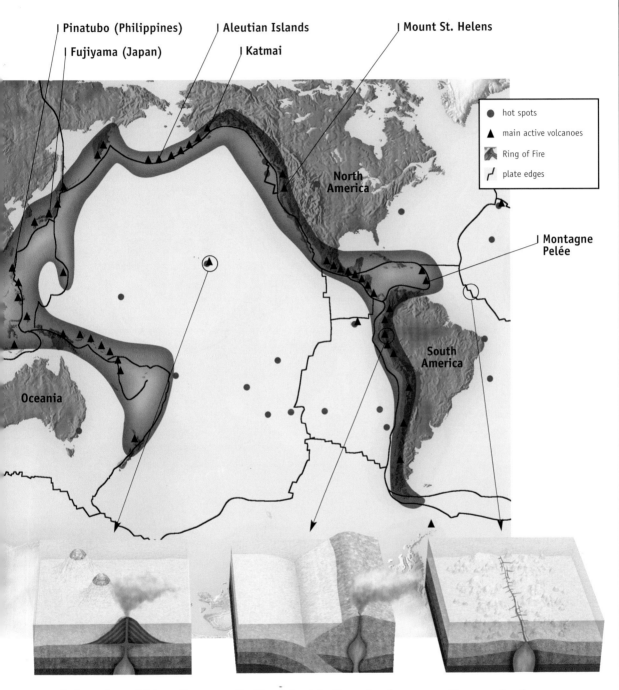

Pinatubo (Philippines)

Fujiyama (Japan)

Aleutian Islands

Katmai

Mount St. Helens

North America

South America

Oceania

Montagne Pelée

- ● hot spots
- ▲ main active volcanoes
- Ring of Fire
- plate edges

Independent of interactions between the plates, **hot spots** occur in the middle of oceanic and continental plates. Pockets of magma rise from the lower mantle of Earth toward the surface, producing volcanic massifs such as Hawaii.

Continental subduction volcanism occurs on the edge of continents, where an oceanic plate and a continental plate meet. Rising magma creates volcanoes such as Cotopaxi along the Andes Cordillera.

Fissure volcanism occurs along oceanic ridges, which extend almost 36,000 miles (60,000 km). In these fragile zones, the spreading of plates allows magma to infiltrate and create long belts of volcanic mountains, such as the one that runs from Iceland to the South Atlantic Ocean.

Volcanic Eruptions

When mountaintops explode

The eruption of a volcano can be compared to a bottle of champagne popping open: the gases dissolved in the magma are the trigger. As the magma rises, the gases are liberated and push upward, increasing the pressure. When the cork pops, the liquid is violently ejected.

When it perforates the surface of Earth, the volcanic eruption forms a crater from which various materials are ejected. Not all volcanoes erupt the same way. The consistency of the magma they contain is partly responsible for how the gases escape and, therefore, the violence of the phenomenon.

SHIELD VOLCANOES

In effusive eruptions, the magma is fluid and the gas it contains escapes easily. Lava spreads in flow or rivers, at a speed of 30 to 60 miles (50 to 100 km) per hour, down the volcano for distances of up to 60 miles (100 km).

Hawaiian eruptions are characterized by abundant lava flows and the ejection of incandescent lava; sometimes, rocks of various sizes are ejected along with the lava flows. In general, effusive volcanoes are round, wide, and flat.

fiery cloud |

STRATOVOLCANOES

Explosive eruptions are the most frightening. The magma is thick and viscous and has a higher gas content. Pressure builds, provoking strong explosions that eject rocks, lava, and gases in every direction.

The eruption produces a cloud that can be dozens of miles (dozens of km) high; debris is violently expelled, and ash may be deposited for hundreds of miles (hundreds of km) around. Volcanoes with explosive eruptions often have steep slopes.

FORMATION OF A CALDERA

Craters more than .6 mile (1 km) in diameter are called calderas. Formed when the top of a volcanic cone collapses, they may be up to 36 miles (60 km) in diameter. During an eruption, magma is ejected from the magma chamber via the central vent and secondary vents ❶. The vents are gradually emptied ❷. The central part of the volcano can no longer support the weight of the volcanic cone, and the top collapses ❸. The cone's material covers the bottom of the caldera, which has very steep sides. Some calderas fill with water and form lakes ❹.

Hot Spots

Volcanoes in a row

At certain specific spots on the planet, pockets of magma from Earth's lower mantle (the layer located above the outer core) rise to the surface very slowly, break through Earth's crust, and produce volcanic massifs in the middle of tectonic plates. These hot spots are immobile; the chains of volcanoes that they create attest to the movement of the tectonic plate above them.

GENERATIONS OF VOLCANOES IN THE OCEAN

Oceanic hot spots create characteristic lines of volcanic islands. When magma rises to the surface, it breaks through the oceanic plate and produces a volcano ❶. The plate moves, but the hot spot stays still. It therefore stops feeding the first volcanic structure and creates a new volcano ❷. The extinct volcano slowly erodes and coral reefs grow on its slopes, forming an atoll — a ring-shaped island around a shallow stretch of water called a lagoon ❸. The eroded volcano, which has sunk below the surface, is called a guyot ❹.

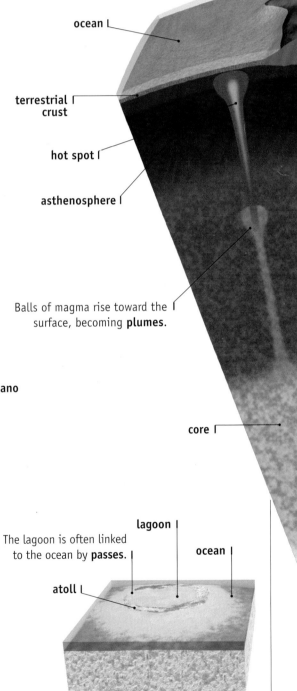

ocean

terrestrial crust

hot spot

asthenosphere

Balls of magma rise toward the surface, becoming **plumes**.

core

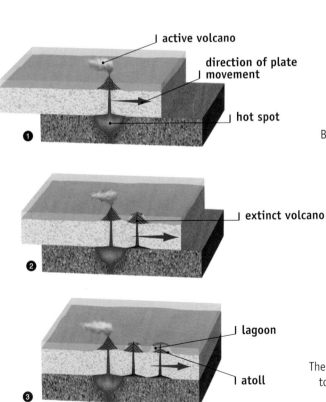

❶ active volcano
direction of plate movement
hot spot

❷ extinct volcano

❸ lagoon
atoll

❹ guyot

The lagoon is often linked to the ocean by **passes**.

lagoon

ocean

atoll

Geysers

When Earth spits up water

Geysers are spectacular water volcanoes that eject immense jets of steam and very hot water, either continuously or intermittently. Most geysers are in volcanic regions where magma is relatively close to the surface of the planet. There are many in Iceland, which gave us the word *geyser* (meaning "to rush forth"), New Zealand, and the United States, where Yellowstone Park has more than 250.

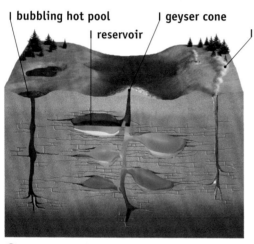

bubbling hot pool | geyser cone

reservoir | fumarole

❶

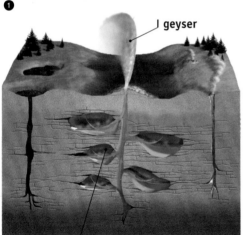

| geyser

❷ steam |

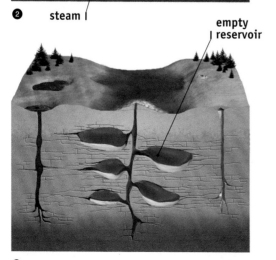

empty reservoir

❸

THE FORMATION OF GEYSERS

Three conditions must be satisfied for geysers to form: the presence of an underground circuit in which the water that percolates into the ground can circulate, then rise to the surface; a reservoir, where this water can accumulate, and a nearby pocket of magma (molten rock), which heats the trapped water.

Water percolates into the ground and accumulates in reservoirs near a pocket of magma ❶. As it is heated, the water slowly turns into steam ❷. The pressure grows, propelling a powerful jet of water and steam toward the surface ❸.

The phenomenon can last from several minutes to several hours. The jet of water subsides when the reservoir contains no more water or steam.

Old Faithful is among the most famous geysers in the world. This geyser in Yellowstone Park is unusually regular: since 1870, it has been spouting thousands of quarts (thousands of liters) of water every fifty to one hundred minutes for about four minutes at a time.

VOLCANIC LANDSCAPES

Aside from geysers, volcanic activity engenders a number of geothermal phenomena. Water and gases in the ground, heated by volcanic rocks, form unusual landscapes featuring flows of mud, water, and vapors.

Gases rise to the surface and form **bubbling hot pools**, where particles of decomposed volcanic rock mix with water.

Water that percolates into the ground near a volcanic zone is heated by the rocks. It rises to the surface at temperatures that are sometimes very high. Many **hot springs** are considered to have therapeutic properties, including those at Bath, in England, and Vichy, in France.

Fumaroles are gas emanations, often found on the flanks of volcanoes. Like geysers, they spurt out from the earth via a vertical conduit in a column of sulfurous steam.

Jets of steam and water spring from the ground, sometimes to a height of more than 300 feet (100 m). The highest active geyser, the Steamboat, whose jet skyrockets over 330 feet (110 m), is in Yellowstone National Park. In the early twentieth century, Wainangu, a geyser in New Zealand, sent water more than 1,450 feet (450 m) into the air.

Mineral deposits form at the foot of the geyser.

Earthquakes

A sudden liberation of energy

Earthquakes take place when the surface of the planet is jolted by a discharge of energy issuing from the depths of Earth. Lithospheric plates move from about .5 inch to 7 inches (1 to 18 cm) per year, and the enormous tension that accumulates at their junctures is directly responsible for seismic activity. Earthquakes therefore take place mainly in volcanic regions and near young mountain ranges, at the edges, or margins, of the plates.

It is estimated that there are almost 1 million earthquakes every year, but only slightly more than 5 percent of them can be felt; the others are of too low a magnitude. When they occur in cities, earthquakes cause terrible disasters, sometimes leading to thousands of deaths.

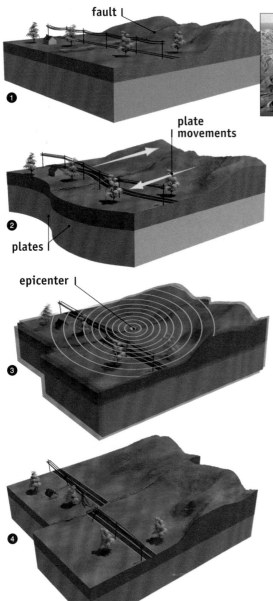

The **San Andreas fault**, in California, is among the best-known fractures in Earth's crust.

HOW AN EARTHQUAKE OCCURS

Earthquakes usually take place along faults in Earth's crust, at the point where two tectonic plates meet ❶.

Plate movements compress and expand the rock, subjecting it to considerable tension and friction. In this stage, the edges of the plates are stuck together and immobile ❷.

When the pressure becomes too great, a huge amount of energy is suddenly released, producing a series of tremors of Earth's crust and vibrations that propagate up to the surface ❸.

Following the earthquake, the affected region undergoes an alteration in form or shape ❹.

Then, little by little, the tensions begin to accumulate again.

The January 1994 earthquake in the area of Los Angeles, California, was devastating.

LOCATING AN EARTHQUAKE

The location of an earthquake is defined by two specific zones: the hypocenter and the epicenter. The hypocenter may be as much as 425 miles (700 km) below the surface. The deeper it is, the greater the distance the waves propagate. However, most earthquakes have a hypocenter less than 12 miles (20 km) below the surface. Each mineral particle oscillates, and this oscillation is transmitted very quickly from one particle to another over very long distances, in a manner similar to concentric circles spreading on the surface of water.

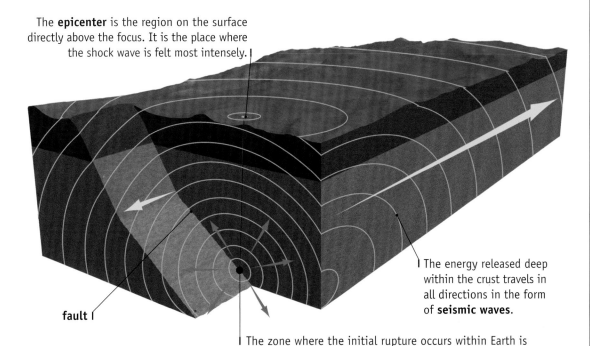

The **epicenter** is the region on the surface directly above the focus. It is the place where the shock wave is felt most intensely.

fault

The energy released deep within the crust travels in all directions in the form of **seismic waves**.

The zone where the initial rupture occurs within Earth is called the **focus** of the earthquake. It is from this point that the energy is suddenly released.

THE RICHTER SCALE		
magnitude	**effects**	**annual frequency**
< 2	micro-earthquake, imperceptible, recorded on local instruments	600,000
2–2.9	potentially perceptible earthquake	300,000
3–3.9	earthquake felt by a few people	50,000
4–4.9	earthquake felt by most people	6,200
5–5.9	moderate earthquake, minor damage caused by shaking	800
6–6.9	important earthquake, damage in inhabited areas	100–300
7–7.9	major earthquake, major damage in inhabited areas	15-20
> 8	very rare earthquake, total destruction in inhabited areas	0–1

There are several methods for calculating the intensity of an earthquake. Some, such as the Mercalli scale, take account of the extent of material damage (such as broken windows and fallen buildings) and require on-site observation.

The Richter scale, invented by U.S. geophysicist Charles Francis Richter, measures the magnitude of an earthquake — that is, the amount of energy released — more precisely. Each whole number in the scale corresponds to a force thirty-two times more powerful than the preceding number. Thus, a magnitude 6 earthquake is thirty-two times more powerful than a magnitude 5 earthquake.

Seismic Waves

When the tension between the plates reaches its maximum, an incredible amount of energy is violently released in the form of shock waves called seismic waves. These waves travel great distances through solid materials, causing vibrations in the rocks.

The intensity of earthquakes is measured with a seismograph, an instrument that measures the horizontal and vertical movements of the ground. A seismogram (the chart produced by the seismograph) gives a portrait of the waves that are shaking our planet. It makes a jagged line, with each peak corresponding to a movement of the ground.

RECORDING VERTICAL MOVEMENTS

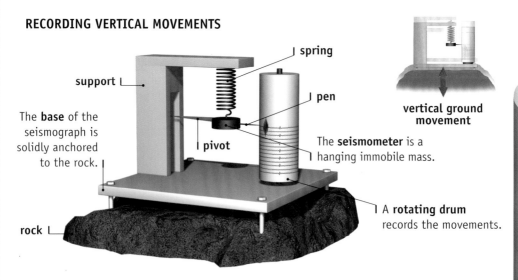

support

The **base** of the seismograph is solidly anchored to the rock.

rock

spring

pen

pivot

The **seismometer** is a hanging immobile mass.

A **rotating drum** records the movements.

vertical ground movement

When an earthquake occurs, the movement of the ground caused by seismic waves is transmitted to the base of the seismograph. The seismometer, like a pendulum, remains still due to inertia so that it serves as an independent reference point in relation to the ground's movement. The pen, connected to the pendulum, records this movement on the rotating drum.

RECORDING HORIZONTAL MOVEMENTS

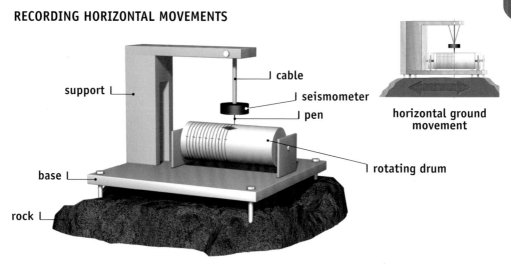

support

base

rock

cable

seismometer

pen

rotating drum

horizontal ground movement

The apparatus used to record horizontal movements works the same way. When the ground moves, the seismograph moves horizontally except for the pendulum, which remains still.

THREE TYPES OF SEISMIC WAVES

Seismic waves produced by an earthquake travel great distances and can be detected at great distances from their origin. Three types of waves travel at different speeds on the surface and through the ground.

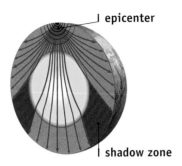

epicenter

shadow zone

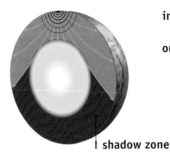

shadow zone

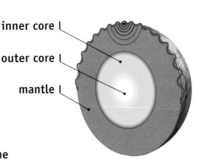

inner core

outer core

mantle

P waves (primary waves) are transmitted through all materials and are the first to be recorded by seismographs. A phenomenon called refraction keeps them from reaching certain regions of the planet, which are called shadow zones.

S waves (secondary waves) propagate only in solid materials and travel more slowly than P waves. They are blocked by Earth's liquid core and leave a larger shadow zone.

When they reach the surface, P and S waves are converted into **L waves** (long waves), which act on the surface only and are the slowest moving of the three.

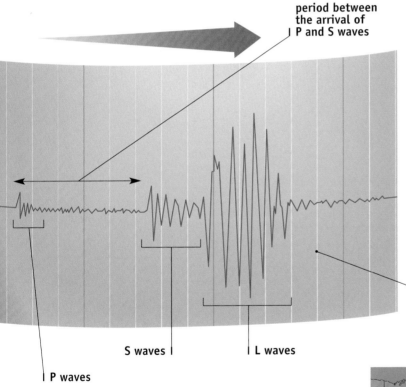

period between the arrival of P and S waves

seismogram

S waves

L waves

P waves

ANALYZING THE SEISMOGRAM

When an earthquake occurs, the ground's oscillations are represented on the seismogram by characteristic waves, which correspond to three types of seismic waves. The distance of the epicenter from the seismograph is determined by measuring the amount of time between when the P waves begin and when the S waves begin.

LOCATING THE EPICENTER

The epicenter of an earthquake can be determined by analyzing data from three stations located at different places.

For precise location, seismologists at each station draw a circle with a radius equivalent to the distance shown on the graph. The point where all three circles intersect is the epicenter.

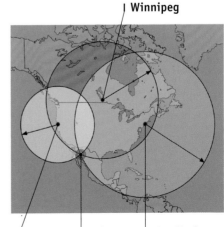

Winnipeg

Berkeley

epicenter

New York

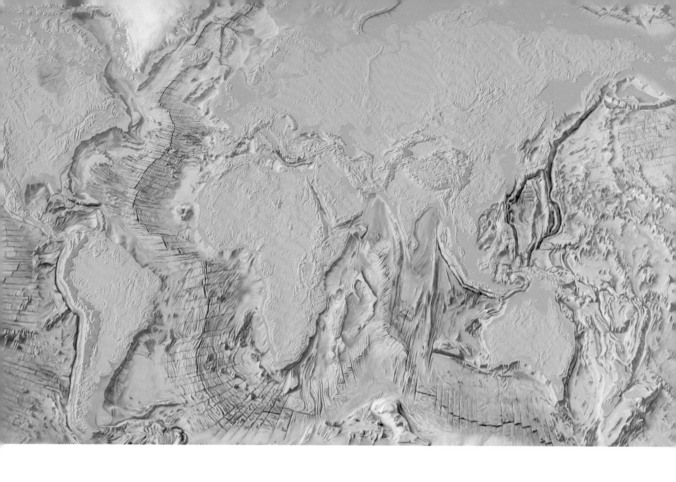

When does a stream become a river? What does the ocean floor look like? Why are there tides? From mountaintops to the abyssal depths, water is present all over our planet; in fact, it covers two-thirds of Earth's surface. The ocean is host to fascinating phenomena, such as ocean currents, tsunamis, and waves, and it is an essential factor in exchanges of energy and materials around the world.

Water and Oceans

44   **Watercourses**
How rivers irrigate the planet

46   **The World's Rivers and Lakes**
Freshwater on Earth's surface

48   **The World Ocean**
Vast bodies of water covering the planet

50   **The Ocean Floor**
Underwater landscapes

52   **Oceanic Trenches and Ridges**
Relief features of the ocean floor

54   **Ocean Currents**
Circulation of oceanic waters

56   **Waves**
A surface phenomenon

58   **Tsunamis**
Gigantic waves

60   **The Tides**
Celestial objects moving the oceans

Watercourses

How rivers irrigate the planet

As it flows from the mountain peaks to the sea, water feeds glaciers, lakes, and rivers. When it arrives in the ocean, it evaporates and forms clouds, which drop rain back into the watercourses. For millions of years, this great hydrologic cycle has formed the landscape by carving out valleys, eroding mountains, and altering shorelines.

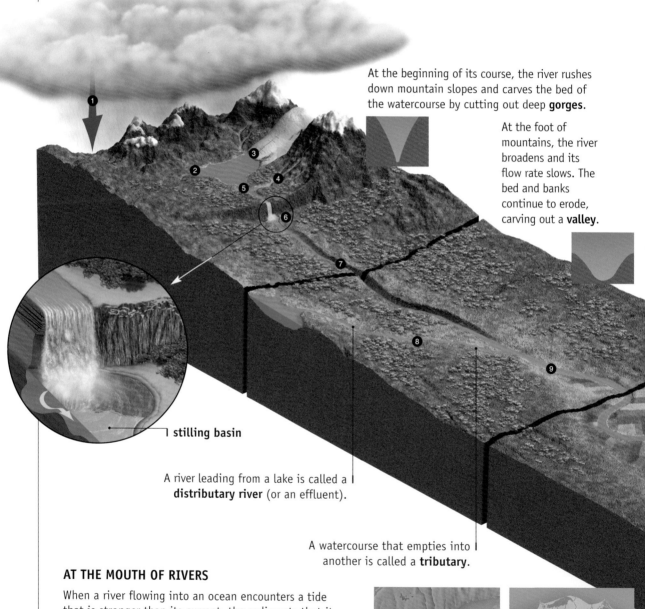

At the beginning of its course, the river rushes down mountain slopes and carves the bed of the watercourse by cutting out deep **gorges**.

At the foot of mountains, the river broadens and its flow rate slows. The bed and banks continue to erode, carving out a **valley**.

stilling basin

A river leading from a lake is called a **distributary river** (or an effluent).

A watercourse that empties into another is called a **tributary**.

AT THE MOUTH OF RIVERS

When a river flowing into an ocean encounters a tide that is stronger than its current, the sediments that it carries are dispersed. The river widens in a funnel shape called an **estuary**.

When a river does not encounter a stronger current, it deposits its sediments at its mouth. The alluvia — the sediment deposits — spread out in a fan shape divided into channels of varying widths and shapes. This is called a **delta**.

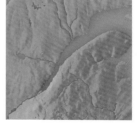

The estuary of the St. Lawrence River, Canada.

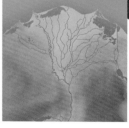

The Nile delta, in Egypt.

DRAINAGE NETWORK

Watercourses (springs, rivers, and lakes) form a drainage basin that is hierarchically arranged: each watercourse empties into a larger one and ultimately into the sea. Drainage basins have different geometrical layouts that vary according to climate, the relief of the landscape, and the nature of the rock. There are a dozen characteristic networks.

Each drainage network is limited by a natural border formed by high-altitude ridges. This is its drainage divide. In North America, this line crosses from north to south along the Rocky Mountains: east of the Rockies, watercourses flow toward the Atlantic; to the west, they flow toward the Pacific.

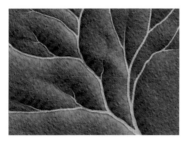

The **dendritic drainage** pattern is one of the most common. It is found in zones where the relief and nature of the rocks are homogeneous.

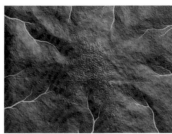

The **radial drainage pattern** is characteristic of mountains, where watercourses diverge from a peak.

The **reticulate drainage pattern**, forming a checkerboard, frequently appears in areas composed of alternating hard and soft rock, often cut into by faults.

FROM THE STREAM TO THE OCEAN

Rainwater ❶ infiltrates into the ground and then rises to the surface in the form of a spring ❷ flowing down hills and mountains. As it is fed by more springs and meltwater from glaciers ❸, it becomes a mountain stream ❹ and then a young river ❺. It continues flowing down the mountain, following steep slopes and forming waterfalls ❻. The river carves out deep gorges ❼, then broadens. Fed by tributaries ❽, it becomes a large river ❾. As it grows wider, the river forms meanders ❿. Often, a delta forms at its mouth ⓫, saturated with the sediments that it has transported, and finally it flows into the ocean ⓬. Water evaporation ⓭ in the oceans forms clouds. The hydrologic cycle starts over.

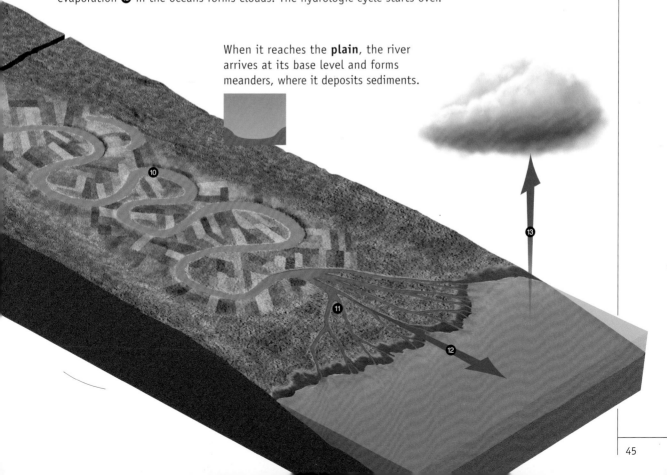

When it reaches the **plain**, the river arrives at its base level and forms meanders, where it deposits sediments.

The World's Rivers and Lakes

Freshwater on Earth's surface

The continents are surrounded by oceans and crisscrossed by vast water systems. Although the quantity of water in the rivers and lakes is minimal (less than 1 percent) compared to the total amount of water on Earth, it still represents a very large volume. Surface water flows down mountains to irrigate valleys and plains everywhere on the planet. A river such as the Amazon receives water from fifteen thousand watercourses. Even desert zones are dotted with oases covering an underground body of water, and some particularly dry areas are supplied by artificial lakes.

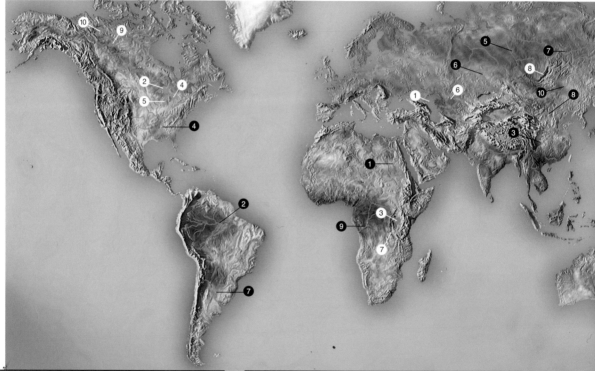

THE LONGEST RIVERS		
	length	
	miles	km
❶ Nile	4,000	6,670
❷ Amazon	3,940	6,570
❸ Yangzi Jiang	3,780	6,300
❹ Mississippi-Missouri	3,580	5,970
❺ Yeniseyskiy-Angara	3,520	5,870
❻ Ob-Irtysh	3,250	5,410
❼ Paraná	2,930	4,880
❽ Huang He	2,900	4,840
❾ Congo	2,780	4,630
❿ Amur	2,660	4,440

THE LARGEST LAKES		
	area	
	square miles	sq km
① Caspian Sea	149,150	386,400
② Lake Superior	31,690	82,100
③ Lake Victoria	26,830	69,500
④ Lake Huron	23,080	59,800
⑤ Lake Michigan	22,290	57,750
⑥ Aral Sea	13,050	33,800
⑦ Lake Tanganyika	12,700	32,900
⑧ Lake Baikal	12,240	31,700
⑨ Great Bear Lake	12,200	31,600
⑩ Great Slave Lake	11,160	28,900

LAKES

Surface water generally flows toward the sea, but sometimes it is held back by a depression or a dam and forms a lake. Although most lakes contain freshwater, some have elevated salinity due to a high rate of evaporation and the accumulation of dissolved mineral salts. The Great Salt Lake in Utah is even saltier than the ocean. Thus, any body of water that is surrounded by land, regardless of its salinity, is classified as a lake.

The water in **lakes of glacial origin** has accumulated in depressions carved out by glaciers and in valleys where moraines as high as 650 feet (200 m) have formed dams. Most lakes in the Northern Hemisphere are of this type.

Tectonic lakes occupy natural basins created by the movement of Earth's crust along folds and faults. Often located below sea level, they sometimes form closed systems, without tributaries.

The craters of some volcanoes are filled with water. **Volcanic lakes** may also form in valleys where hardened lava flows hold back the water.

Oxbow lakes sometimes appear in the areas around rivers. They are formed in meanders, or oxbows, abandoned by the watercourse. Unless they are regularly fed by new water, they rapidly dry up.

An **oasis** is formed in deserts when the wind erodes the ground and exposes the water table. Oases also appear where a fault line causes water to flow toward a particular point.

WATER DISTRIBUTION

oceans (97.2%)

freshwater (2.8%)

glaciers and icebergs (77%)

groundwater (22%)

surface water (rivers, lakes, and atmosphere) (1%)

Reservoirs, artificial lakes whose waters are usually held in by dams, supply water for human consumption, irrigation, or production of hydro-electric power.

The World Ocean

Vast bodies of water covering the planet

Only 30 percent of Earth's surface is exposed land. The rest is covered by the world ocean, a huge mass of saltwater measuring 97.2 percent of the planet's water. This enormous mass of water is divided by the continents into four main regions (the Pacific, Atlantic, Indian, and Arctic oceans) and many smaller basins, some of them shallow and situated inland — the seas. Some saltwater lakes, although they are landlocked and have no link with the world ocean, are also classified as seas, such as the Caspian Sea and the Dead Sea.

THE OCEAN'S TEMPERATURE

The temperature of seawater depends on the season and the latitude, but especially on the depth. Surface water ❶, heated by solar radiation, has an average temperature of 77° F to 82° F (25° C to 28° C) at the equator, 54° F to 63° F (12° C to 17° C) in temperate zones, and only 30° F to 39° F (–1° C to 4° C) in polar regions. The middle layer of water is called the thermocline ❷. It is a transitional zone, where the decrease in luminosity causes a sudden drop in temperature to 40° F (5° C). Finally, in the deepest zone ❸, the temperature is always about the same, varying only from 32° F to 39° F (0° C to 4° C) at all latitudes and in all seasons.

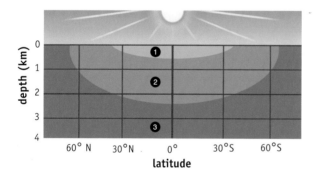

COMPOSITION OF SEAWATER

The salinity of ocean water varies from one place to another but is generally between 3.2 percent and 3.7 percent. In tropical regions, higher temperatures and a lower precipitation rate favor water evaporation and thus a greater concentration of salt. On the other hand, in temperate regions, where temperatures are lower and precipitation more abundant, the water is less salty.

Seawater contains almost all of the chemical elements known, including chlorine, sodium, sulfur, magnesium, and calcium.

North Pacific
Ocean

South Pacific
Ocean

water (96.5%)

salinity (3.5%)

chlorine (55%)

sodium (30.6%)

other elements (0.7%)

potassium (1.1%)

calcium (1.2%)

magnesium (3.7%)

sulfur (7.7%)

EARTH'S MAIN OCEANS AND SEAS

1. Bering Sea
2. Gulf of Alaska
3. Beaufort Sea
4. Hudson Bay
5. Labrador Sea
6. Gulf of Mexico
7. Caribbean Sea
8. Weddell Sea
9. Greenland Sea
10. Norwegian Sea
11. North Sea
12. Baltic Sea
13. Adriatic Sea
14. Black Sea
15. Mediterranean Sea
16. Red Sea
17. Persian Gulf
18. Gulf of Oman
19. Bay of Bengal
20. China Sea
21. Philippine Sea
22. Sea of Japan
23. Sea of Okhotsk
24. Coral Sea
25. Tasman Sea
26. Ross Sea

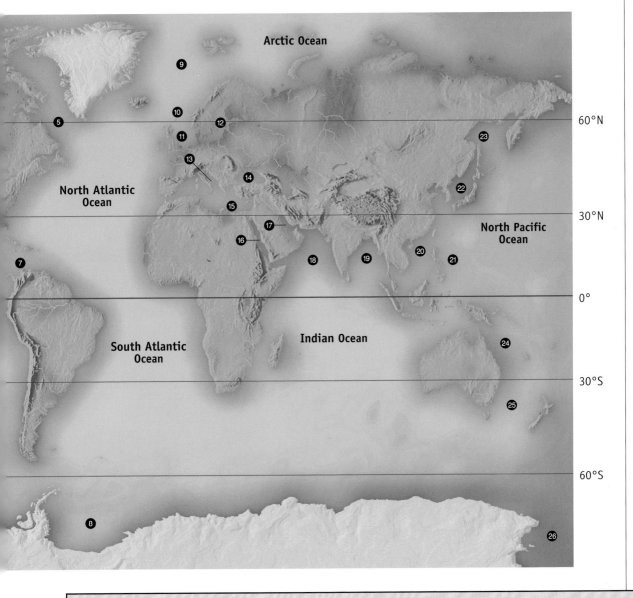

ocean	area	volume
Pacific	63,700,000 mi² (165,000,000 km²)	170,000,000 mi³ (707,000,000 km³)
Atlantic	31,800,000 mi² (82,400,000 km²)	5,700,000 mi³ (23,600,000 km³)
Indian	23,300,000 mi² (73,400,000 km²)	70,000,000 mi³ (292,000,000 km³)
Arctic	5,400,000 mi² (14,000,000 km²)	4,000,000 mi³ (16,700,000 km³)

The Ocean Floor

It is difficult to imagine that the mountains and valleys that we see on land also exist on the seafloor. In fact, the ocean depths have a much wider range of relief features than we might believe. Mountains, plains, plateaus, volcanoes, trenches, and canyons form astounding landscapes on the seafloor that are very similar to those on land — except that some are much bigger than anything on the continents.

The **continental shelf** lies just off the continental coasts. It is an underwater extension of the continent, covered with sediments. The shelf extends anywhere from .6 mile to 600 miles (1 to 1,000 km). It generally slopes gently downward to depths of 500 to 650 feet (150 to 200 m).

The **continental slope** forms the real border between the continent and the ocean. From the edge of the continental shelf, it drops abruptly to more than 9,750 feet (3,000 m) in depth.

canyon

Sediments flowing from the canyons form **fans**.

Guyots are volcanoes whose summits have been eroded.

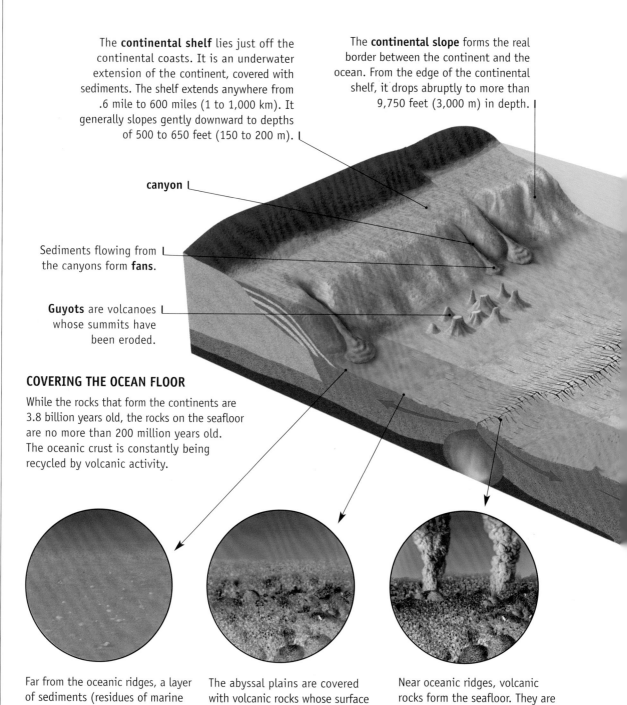

COVERING THE OCEAN FLOOR

While the rocks that form the continents are 3.8 billion years old, the rocks on the seafloor are no more than 200 million years old. The oceanic crust is constantly being recycled by volcanic activity.

Far from the oceanic ridges, a layer of sediments (residues of marine organisms, sand, volcanic dust, and rubble) as thick as 1,600 feet (500 m) covers the sea floor.

The abyssal plains are covered with volcanic rocks whose surface has been worn and rounded by time. Sediments begin to accumulate in these areas.

Near oceanic ridges, volcanic rocks form the seafloor. They are not yet covered with sediments.

THE BIRTH OF AN OCEAN

Although we can't see it, the oceans are constantly coming into existence on the planet. This process, which takes tens of millions of years, begins when two continental plates spread apart and magma wells up through the fissures ❶. The ocean crust gets thinner, bulges, and then sinks, forming a rift valley ❷. Water gradually flows into the new valley ❸ as the divergence continues. Accumulating lava forms new oceanic crust, while the old crust is pushed outward. Along the fissure zone, the crust folds like a carpet to form new mountains at the bottom of the ocean ❹.

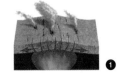

❶

❷

❸

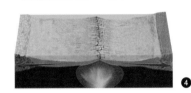

❹

Most of the seafloor consists of vast **abyssal plains** composed of oceanic crust. Generally at a depth of about 10,000 feet (3,000 m), these plains sometimes descend as deep as 20,000 feet (6,000 m), but the slope is so gentle that it is almost imperceptible.

oceanic ridge

marine mountain

sea level

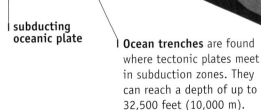

island arc

subducting oceanic plate

Ocean trenches are found where tectonic plates meet in subduction zones. They can reach a depth of up to 32,500 feet (10,000 m).

Among the most stunning formations on the ocean floor are **volcanoes**, some of which rise above sea level to form islands.

Oceanic Trenches and Ridges

Relief features of the ocean floor

The seafloor is not completely flat. Immense mountain belts called oceanic ridges stretch for almost 43,500 miles (70,000 km) across the abyssal plains! With altitudes of between 3,250 and 9,750 feet (1,000 and 3,000 m), these underwater mountains are sharply defined along their entire length by a rift valley, a central plain of subsidence, which forms as the oceanic plates spread apart. Where tectonic plates meet, gigantic oceanic depressions called trenches reach depths comparable to the altitude of the highest peaks on the continents.

Some of the underwater mountains of the mid-Atlantic ridge break the surface to form imposing islands such as **Iceland.**

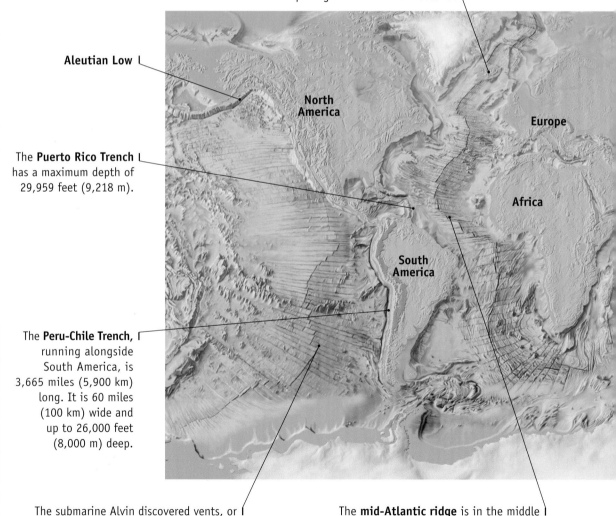

Aleutian Low

North America

Europe

The **Puerto Rico Trench** has a maximum depth of 29,959 feet (9,218 m).

Africa

South America

The **Peru-Chile Trench,** running alongside South America, is 3,665 miles (5,900 km) long. It is 60 miles (100 km) wide and up to 26,000 feet (8,000 m) deep.

The submarine Alvin discovered vents, or "black smokers," near the **East Pacific Rise**. These natural vents, which spew iron sulfide at more than 520° F (270° C), are up to 65 feet (20 m) in height.

The **mid-Atlantic ridge** is in the middle of the Atlantic Ocean, midway between the Americas, Europe, and Africa.

EXPLORING THE DEPTHS

Since William Beebe made the first bathysphere in the 1930s, a number of vehicles have been built to explore the oceans. They have dived to increasing depths and are now reaching extreme depths. The bathyscaph Trieste has held the diving record since 1960.

The **Mariana Trench**, in the northwest Pacific, reaches a depth of 35,861 feet (11,034 m). It could easily hold Mount Everest, with an altitude of 28,756 feet (8,848 m). This trench is the deepest spot in the world.

The deepest point of the **Philippine Trench** is 34,125 feet (10,500 m).

Java Trench

Asia

Australia

Southwest Indian Ridge

The **Carlsberg Ridge** meets Africa's Great Rift Valley in the Gulf of Aden.

Cousteau's SP 350 diving saucer
1,140 ft (350 m)

Beebe's bathysphere
3,000 ft (923 m)

Barton's benthoscope
4,453 ft (1,370 m)

9,750 ft (3,000 m)

Cousteau's SP 3000 diving saucer
10,888 ft (3,350 m)

Alvin submarine
14,625 ft (4,500 m)

19,500 ft (6,000 m)

Underwater exploration has enabled scientists to discover unusual animal species, like the deep-sea anglerfish, which uses luminous bacteria to attract its prey.

Shinkai submersible
21,125 ft (6,500 m)

Southeast Indian Ridge

29,250 ft (9,000 m)

Trieste bathyscaph
35,464 ft (10,912 m)

Mariana Trench

35,861 ft (11,034 m)

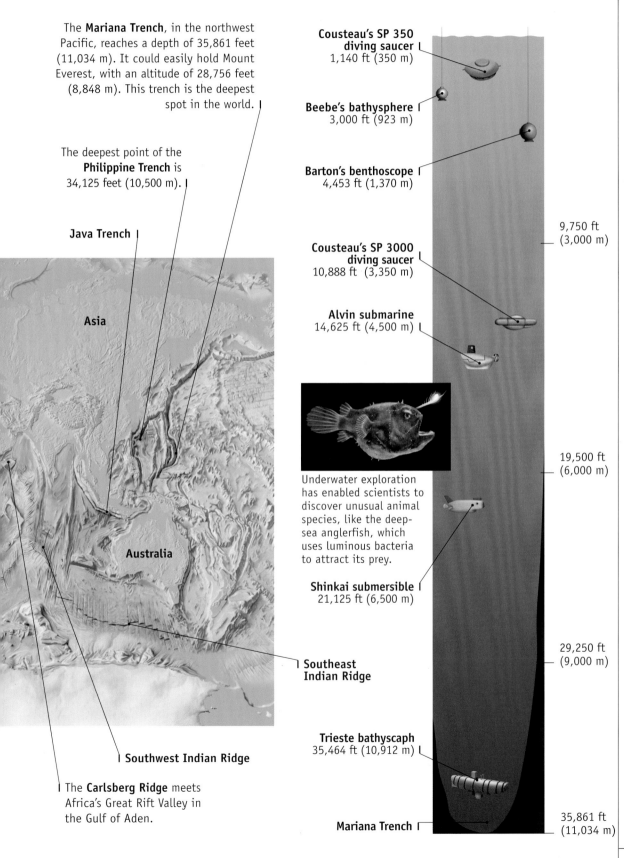

Ocean Currents

Circulation of oceanic waters

The winds that sweep the surface of the oceans give rise to powerful currents. Air pressure causes water molecules to move first on the surface, then deeper in the ocean, resulting in mass movements of water along very precise paths. This planetary mixing of waters supplies oxygen to the oceans. It also sometimes causes serious climatic changes; one example is the cyclical warm El Niño current, which is responsible for torrential rains in South America and drought in Asia.

SURFACE CURRENTS AND DEEP CURRENTS

The currents that move through the upper layers of the oceans are warm currents. Deep currents, which are much colder, are created by variations in density between masses of water.

In the polar zones, melting ice drains salt toward the bottom of the ocean. These polar waters, colder and saltier than equatorial waters, sink under the warm currents and flow toward the equator, moderating the overall temperature of waters and the climate. As it circulates, the water slowly heats up and gradually rises toward the surface.

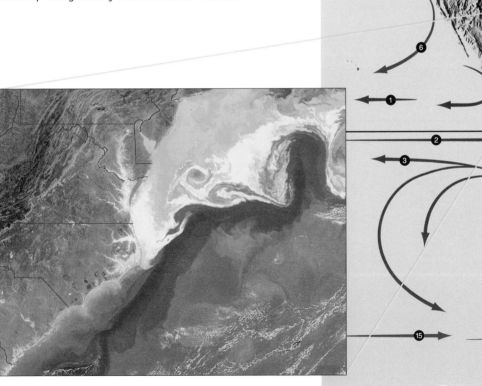

THE GULF STREAM

Among the currents generated by dominant winds, the Gulf Stream is by far the best known. Like the Brazil Current, it originates near the equator, where the trade winds blow, but while the Brazil Current moves toward the Southern Hemisphere, the Gulf Stream moves north, then northeast. It is 35 miles (60 km) wide and at least 1,950 feet (600 m) deep and flows at a rate of 75 miles (120 km) per day.

The satellite image (above) shows how the waters of the Gulf Stream (colored red and yellow) warm the climate up to the high latitudes.

THE INFLUENCE OF EARTH'S ROTATION

The paths of ocean currents do not exactly follow the directions of the winds because they are deflected by the Coriolis force, a phenomenon generated by Earth's rotation. The Coriolis effect causes currents generally to curve to the right in the Northern Hemisphere and to the left in the Southern Hemisphere.

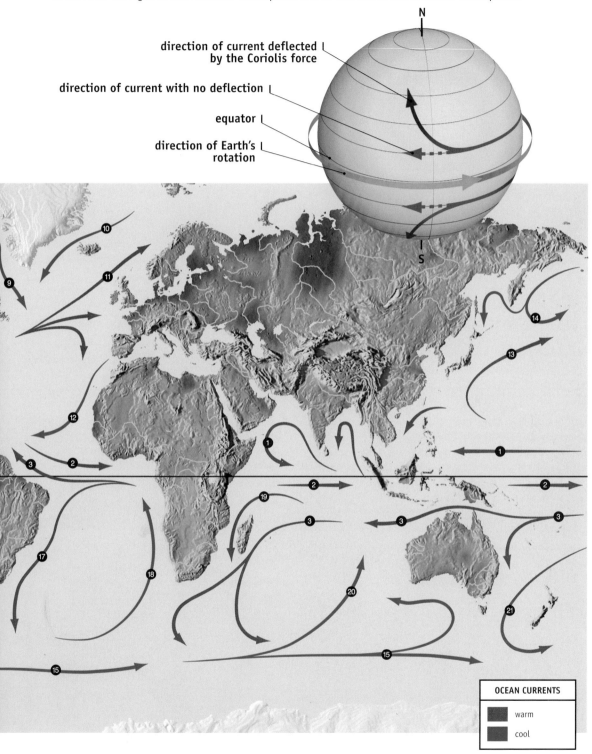

direction of current deflected by the Coriolis force

direction of current with no deflection

equator

direction of Earth's rotation

N

S

OCEAN CURRENTS

warm

cool

MAIN OCEAN CURRENTS

1. North Equatorial Current
2. Equatorial Countercurrent
3. South Equatorial Current
4. North Pacific Drift
5. Alaska Current
6. California Current
7. Caribbean Current
8. Gulf Stream
9. Labrador Current
10. Greenland Current
11. North Atlantic Drift
12. Canary Current
13. Kuroshio
14. Oyashio
15. Antarctic Current
16. Peru Current
17. Brazil Current
18. Benguela Current
19. Agulhas Current
20. West Australia Current
21. East Australia Current

Waves

A surface phenomenon

What is responsible for the never-ending succession of waves breaking on the shore? Contrary to what one might believe, waves are not produced by massive water movements. Although an optical illusion suggests that water is traveling en masse from the open sea toward the coast, a wave is simply a form produced by movements on the water surface caused by the wind. Waves break when they reach the shore.

The strength of the wind, how long it blows, and its fetch (the stretch of water over which it blows without meeting an obstacle) determine the size of waves. The highest wave ever was observed in the Pacific Ocean in 1933: it was 110 feet (34 m) high.

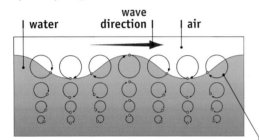

PARTICLES IN ROTATION

In a wave, the only moving particles of water are those agitated by the pressure difference caused by the wind. These particles move very little horizontally, but they move in a circle, with a diameter equal to the height of the wave, that is completed as the crest of each wave passes.

circular movement of particles

HOW WAVES BREAK

Agitated by the wind, particles of water roll on the surface, and a wave-form oscillation of water is propagated ❶. The waves continue as long as the wind does not weaken and no obstacle impedes them. When the swell reaches the coast, it is slowed by the rise in level of the seafloor ❷ and the waves change in shape. The crests get closer together ❸ and the wavelength diminishes, although the period (the interval of time between two crests) remains the same. The waves get taller ❹ and the movement of the water particles becomes elliptical ❺. When they can no longer move in this way, the wave breaks. Energy is dispersed as the particles are ejected forward ❻ in a rush of foam.

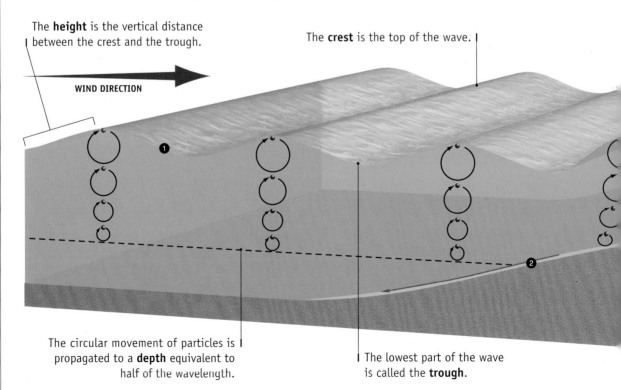

The **height** is the vertical distance between the crest and the trough.

The **crest** is the top of the wave.

WIND DIRECTION

The circular movement of particles is propagated to a **depth** equivalent to half of the wavelength.

The lowest part of the wave is called the **trough**.

EXTRAORDINARY WAVES

The longer a wave propagates without encountering an obstacle, the more powerful it becomes. The shores of Oahu, in Hawaii, receive extraordinary waves, often reaching more than 30 feet (10 m) in height. They are born off the Aleutian Islands, near Alaska, and are slowed only by the underwater continental shelf when they arrive.

A BOTTLE IN THE OCEAN

Unless it is pushed by a current or the wind, a bottle thrown into the sea moves very little in any direction: it simply follows the circular movement of the water particles.

Carried by the movement of the swell, it rises on the crest ❶, moves forward ❷, descends into the trough ❸, moves backward as a new wave approaches ❹, and rises once again to its original position as a new crest arrives ❺.

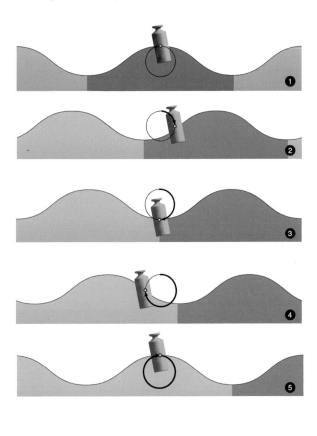

The **swell** is the movement of waves in the open sea, before they break.

The **wavelength** is the horizontal distance between two successive crests.

Waves unfurling into foam on the shore are called **breakers**.

The wave subsides and sinks back into the sea, creating an **undertow**.

For a short time before it breaks on the shore, the crest forms a **comber** (tube of air).

Tsunamis

Gigantic waves

Tsunamis are series of giant waves that hit the coastlines. Caused by geologic incidents on the ocean floor (earthquakes, underwater volcanic eruptions, landslides), they are very different from waves produced by surface phenomena such as hurricanes and storms. The term "tidal wave" is better known but inaccurate, since the phenomenon has nothing to do with the tides. The volume of water displaced and the energy resulting from tsunamis are immense, which explains why they generally cause more deaths than do volcanic eruptions and earthquakes. In 1958, a landslide in Alaska produced a wave with the exceptional height of 1,690 feet (520 m)!

HOW A TSUNAMI DEVELOPS

A geologic incident on the ocean floor, at a depth of thousands of yards (thousands of m), causes part of the ocean floor to sink or rise ❶. A shock wave ❷ creates enormous waves ❸ that move at a velocity of 375 to 500 miles (600 to 800 km) per hour. This velocity is proportional to the depth and diminishes as the tsunami nears the coast; the gradual upward slope of the ocean floor ❹ increases the height of the waves. When the ocean floor becomes shallow, the swell is deformed; the waves slow to about 30 miles (50 km) per hour, but their height ❺ grows considerably. Finally, these giant waves ❻ break on the shore.

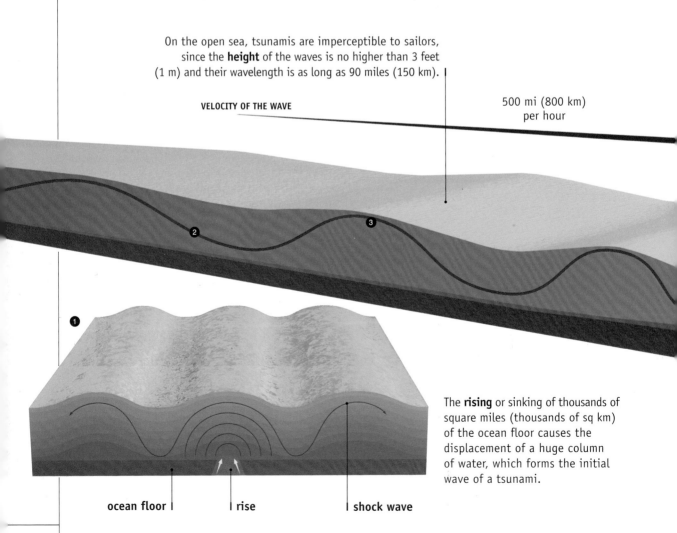

On the open sea, tsunamis are imperceptible to sailors, since the **height** of the waves is no higher than 3 feet (1 m) and their wavelength is as long as 90 miles (150 km).

VELOCITY OF THE WAVE

500 mi (800 km) per hour

The **rising** or sinking of thousands of square miles (thousands of sq km) of the ocean floor causes the displacement of a huge column of water, which forms the initial wave of a tsunami.

ocean floor | rise | shock wave

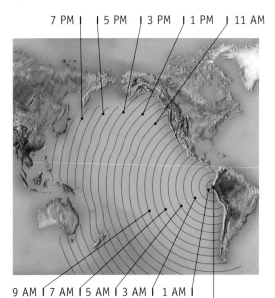

7 PM | 5 PM | 3 PM | 1 PM | 11 AM

9 AM | 7 AM | 5 AM | 3 AM | 1 AM |
earthquake in Ecuador |

An earthquake in Ecuador can cause a tsunami that will travel for more than twenty hours to hit Japan at full strength.

DANGER! TSUNAMI ALERT!

Although tsunamis occur in all oceans, most take place in the Pacific. The geologic activity of the underwater faults associated with the Pacific Ring of Fire makes that region more favorable to the formation of tsunamis. The risk varies as a function of the topography of the ocean floor and the shoreline: bays and peninsulas increase the height of tsunami waves, while coral reefs in the open sea tend to dissipate their power.

Tsunamis travel for many hours before reaching the coast, and a number of countries bordering the Pacific Ocean cooperate to provide constant surveillance of the seafloor. The data recorded by seismographs are transmitted via satellite to the International Tsunami Warning System in Hawaii.

A wave reaching up to 100 feet (30 m) in height (the height of a 10-story building) dumps a **wall of water** with incredible force on the shore, devastating everything in its path. |

On the beach, the first sign of a tsunami is the sudden **receding** of water. When this happens, people must flee to the heights as quickly as possible. Boats near shore must head for the open sea immediately. |

190 mi (300 km) per hour

30 mi (50 km) per hour

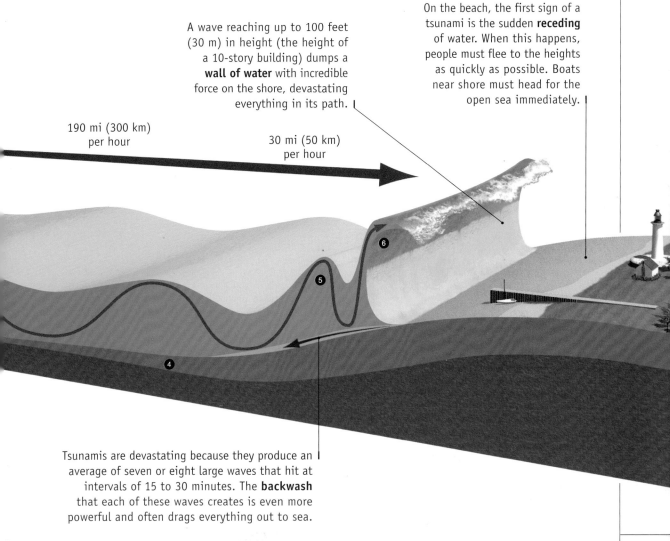

Tsunamis are devastating because they produce an average of seven or eight large waves that hit at intervals of 15 to 30 minutes. The **backwash** that each of these waves creates is even more powerful and often drags everything out to sea.

The Tides

All celestial objects in the Universe exert a mutual attractive force on other bodies that varies according to their respective masses and the distances between them. This fundamental law of physics, gravitational attraction, explains why the oceans of Earth rise and drop several feet (several m) twice a day. Tides are the concrete effect of the attraction exerted by the Moon and the Sun on Earth.

Because it is the celestial object closest to our planet, the Moon plays a greater role in tidal movements, but the Sun, with its very large mass, also has a perceptible effect: it is estimated that its attractive force on ocean waters is 46 percent that of the Moon's.

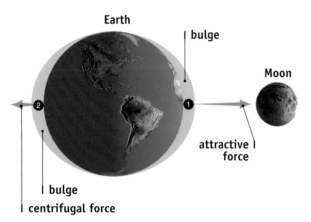

Earth
bulge
Moon
❷
❶
attractive force
bulge
centrifugal force

THE MOON'S FORCE OF ATTRACTION

Even though the Moon is 235,000 miles (378,000 km) away from Earth, it exerts a strong enough gravitational force to move the oceans. When Earth rotates so that a mass of water is facing the Moon, water rises in its direction: this bulge produces a high tide ❶. At the same time, the Moon's gravitational pull on water on the other side of Earth is much weaker. This water is affected by the centrifugal force created by the rotation of the Earth-Moon system and also tends to bulge outward, creating another high tide ❷. If Earth were made only of rigid materials, it would still be deformed by the action of these two forces and would be egg shaped.

Gravitational attraction is not the only influence on the tides: many factors linked to local geography have been discovered. While closed seas are almost unaffected by the phenomenon, the **Bay of Fundy**, on Canada's Atlantic coast, has the greatest tidal variations in the world, with an amplitude (range between low and high tides) of up to 50 feet (16 m).

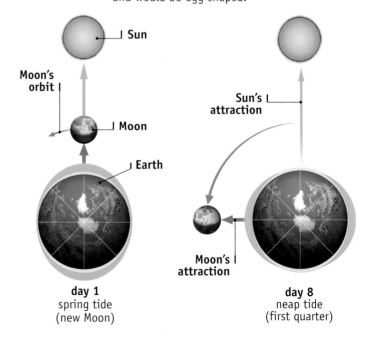

Sun

Moon's orbit
Moon

Earth

day 1
spring tide
(new Moon)

Sun's attraction

Moon's attraction

day 8
neap tide
(first quarter)

DAILY TIDES

At all times, Earth has two high-tide regions, corresponding to bulge zones somewhere on the planet, separated by two low-tide zones. During a single day, every part of the world ocean passes through these four zones. Because the duration of Earth's rotation in relation to the Moon is not 24 hours, but 24 hours and 50 minutes, there are about 6 hours 12 minutes between a high tide and a low tide.

Earth's inclination in relation to the ecliptic (the plane of Earth's orbit), which is 23.5°, also has an effect on the level of high tides. At high latitudes, there is a marked difference between the first high tide of the day, which is relatively low ❶, and the second, which follows 12 hours and 25 minutes later and is much higher ❷.

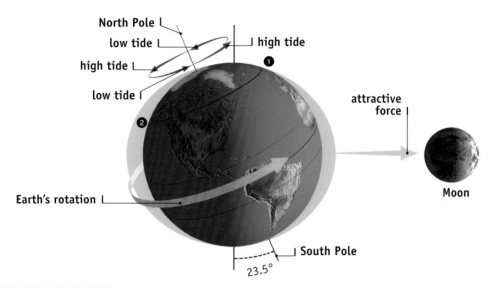

SPRING TIDE, NEAP TIDE

Because the Sun is much farther away than the Moon, its gravitational force as felt on Earth is much weaker than that of the Moon, but it still plays an important role in the tide phenomenon. When the three celestial objects are aligned — that is, on the days of the full Moon and new Moon — the gravitational forces of the Sun and Moon are combined to produce higher-amplitude tides, which are called spring tides.

Conversely, the influences of the Sun and the Moon partially cancel each other out during the middle stages of the lunar cycle (first and last quarters), when the two celestial objects exert perpendicular forces on Earth. At these times there are neap tides, and the tidal swell is weak.

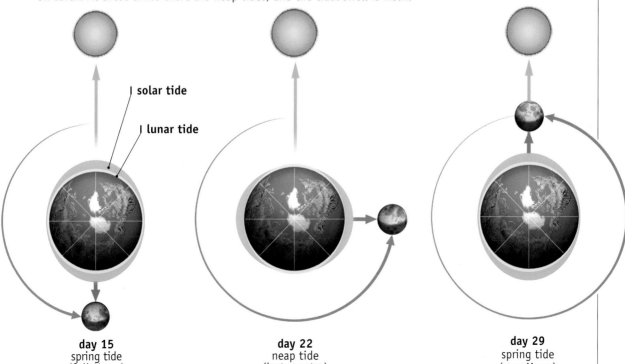

day 15
spring tide
(full Moon)

day 22
neap tide
(last quarter)

day 29
spring tide
(new Moon)

Water and Oceans

Glossary

abyssal: Of or pertaining to the ocean depths.

aggregate: A cluster of distinct elements held together by a solid material.

alluvia: Solid materials (sand, gravel, silt, pebbles) transported and deposited by a watercourse.

amplitude: Difference between the two extreme values of a variable phenomenon, such as temperature, tides, and waves.

archipelago: Group of islands.

continental margin: Underwater region on the edge of a continent between the coast and the oceanic depths.

convection: Transference of heat accompanying the circulation of a fluid (gaseous or liquid).

cordillera: Long, narrow mountain range in South America or Australia.

effluent: A stream flowing out of a lake or other body of water; the outflow or discharge from a stream or other body of water.

epoch: A unit of geologic time; subdivision of a period.

fault: A break or displacement in the continuity of a rock formation, caused by a shifting of the planet's crust.

geographic pole: The two points on Earth (North Pole and South Pole) through which the planet's axis of rotation passes.

geologic time: The period from when Earth was formed to the appearance of writing, which marked the beginning of the historical period.

island arc: Group of volcanic islands aligned parallel to a submarine trench.

isthmus: Narrow strip of land between two stretches of water, connecting two larger landmasses.

magnitude: Measurement of the amount of energy released during an earthquake and its representation on a numeric scale.

massif: A group of mountains, often made of ancient bedrock, that may take various shapes, such as volcanic formations, plateaus, or severely eroded elements.

oceanic trench: Narrow depression in the ocean floor, several thousand miles (several thousand km) long and between 16,500 and 36,000 feet (5,000 and 11,000 m) deep.

oscillation: A single swing in one direction of a body that vibrates, swings, or moves back and forth.

plain: A vast stretch of relatively flat land, at a lower elevation than the relief features in the environs, with slightly hollowed valleys.

plate tectonics: A branch of geology that deals with seismic activity and continental movement. Plate tectonics is based on the theory that the surface of Earth is made up of several large sections that float on Earth's mantle, with seismic activity occurring at points where these sections, or plates, meet.

pyroclast: Debris from a volcanic explosion.

relief: All unevenness, such as depressions and elevations, in the topographic surface of a region.

rift valley: Large, elongated depression with steep side slopes, formed by the subsidence of a block of land between two faults.

salinity: The proportion of salt dissolved in a medium. The salt contained in seawater comes from minerals transported by rivers.

sediments: Solid mineral materials, such as rock, sand, or mud, that have been scraped away from their original location and transported by water, ice, or wind to be deposited in another location. Organic materials may also form sediments.

submarine canyon: Underwater gorge carved into the continental shelf by currents from large rivers or by landslides.

trade winds: Winds that blow steadily from east to west in the intertropical zone, especially above the Pacific and Atlantic oceans.

watercourse: A waterway; the bed or channel created by a waterway.

Books

Beneath Our Feet: The Rocks of Planet Earth. R. H. Vernon (Cambridge University Press)

Earth from Above. Yann Arthus-Bertrand and Sophie Bessis (Harry N. Abrams)

Earth from Above: Using Color-Coded Satellite Images to Examine the Global Environment. Claire L. Parkinson (University Science Books)

Petrology: Igneous, Sedimentary, and Metamorphic. Harvey Blatt and Robert Tracy (W. H. Freeman Co.)

Reading the Earth: Landforms in the Making. Jerome Wyckoff (Adastra West, Inc.)

The Rockhound's Handbook. James R. Mitchell (Gem Guides Book Co.)

Rocks & Minerals (DK Handbooks). Chris Pellant, Harry Taylor (photographer) (D. K. Publishing)

A Short History of Planet Earth: Mountains, Mammals, Fire and Ice (Wiley Popular Science). J. D. MacDougall (John Wiley & Sons)

Volcano Cowboys : The Rocky Evolution of a Dangerous Science. Dick Thompson (St. Martin's Press)

Windows into the Earth: The Geologic Story of Yellowstone and Grand Teton National Parks. Robert Baer Smith and Lee J. Siegel (Oxford University Press)

Videos

The Day the Earth Caught Fire. Val Guest (Anchor Bay)

Journey to the Center of the Earth. Henry Levin (Fox CBS)

Nova: Earthquake. (WGB)

Nova: Volcanoes of the Deep. (WGB)

Standard Deviants: Geology Part I. Richard Diecchio (Cerebellum Corp.)

Standard Deviants: Geology Part II. Richard Diecchio (Cerebellum Corp.)

Volcanoes of the United States. Laurence J. Janksowski (Physical Geography Series)

Web Sites

Geology with Andrew Alden
www.geology.about.com/science/geology

Geologylink
www.geologylink.com

Yahooligans! Geology
www.yahooligans.com/Science_and_Nature/The_Earth/Geology/

USGS: The Learning Web
www.usgs.gov/education/

Index

A

abyssal plain, 50, 51
Africa 52
Alaska 57
Aleutian Islands 52, 57
alluvia 44
Amazon River 46
Amur River 46
Aral Sea 46
Arctic Ocean 48, 49
Asia 54
asthenosphere 35
Atlantic Ocean 48, 49
atoll 35
Australia 28

B

backwash 59
Bay of Fundy 60
Beebe, William 53
"black smokers" 52
Brazil 54
Brazil Current 54
breaker 57
bubbling hot pool 37

C

calderas 34
California 24, 38
Caspian Sea 46, 48
comber 57
Congo River 46
continental drift 28, 29
continental shelf 50
continental slope 50
Coriolis force 55
currents 54, 55

D

Dead Sea 48
delta 44
distributary river 44
dyke 30

E

Earth, composition of 10, 14, 15
Earth, formation of 6, 7
earthquakes 22, 38, 40, 59
Ecuador 59
epicenter 39, 41
eruptive column 30
estuary 44

F

fan 50
freshwater 46
fumaroles 30, 37

G

geologic time scale 8, 9
geysers 30, 32, 36, 37
Great Bear Lake 46
Great Lakes 46
Gulf Stream 54
guyot 35, 50

H

Hawaii 21, 31, 49, 57, 59
Himalayas 7, 17, 25, 29
hot springs 37
Huang He River 46
hypocenter 39

I

Iceland 52
igneous rock 18, 19, 20, 21
India 40, 55
Indian Ocean 48, 49

J

Japan 59
Java Trench 53

L

laccolith 31
lapilli 31
lava 7, 31
Lake Baikal 46
Lake Huron 46
Lake Michigan 46
Lake Superior 46
Lake Tanganyika 46
Lake Victoria 46
Los Angeles 38

M

magma 19
Mariana Trench 53
metamorphic rock 18, 19, 20, 21
Mississippi River 46
Mohs scale 17
Mount Etna 33
Mount Everest 53
(Mount) Fujiyama 33
Mount Kilauea 31
Mount Kilimanjaro 24
Mount Krakatoa 32
Mount Pinatubo 31, 39
Mount St. Helens 33
Mount Vesuvius 33

N

Nile River 44, 46

O

oasis 47
Ob-Irtysh 46
Old Faithful geyser 36
oxbow lakes 47

P

Pacific Ocean 48, 49, 52, 53, 56
Pangaea 4, 7, 26, 28
Parana River 46
Peru-Chile Trench 52
Philippine Trench 53
plate tectonics 24, 25, 28
Puerto Rico Trench 52

R

reservoir 36, 47
Richter, Francis 39
Richter Scale 39

S

St. Lawrence River 44
salinity 48
San Andreas fault 24, 38
seawater 48
sedimentary rock 18, 19, 20, 21
seismic waves 40, 41
seismogram 40
seismograph 40
seismometer 40
sill 30
South America 54
swell 57

T

tectonic lake 47
tributary 44
Trieste bathyscaph 53
tsunamis 58, 59

UVW

undertow 57
volcanic bombs 31
volcanism 32, 33
volcanoes 18, 19, 30, 31, 32, 33, 34, 35, 51
Wainangu geyser 37
watercourses 44, 45
wavelength 57
Wegener, Alfred 26

XYZ

Yangzi Jiang River 46
Yellowstone 36, 37
Yeniseyskiy-Angara River 46